LONGER LASTING MASTERY

A PRACTICAL GUIDE FOR MEN AND WOMEN TO PROLONGING THEIR LOVEMAKING.

TATIANA PERERA

SWEETSPIRE LITERATURE
——— MANAGEMENT ———

Table of Contents

MY BELIEFS AND WHAT INSPIRES ME

Healing energy is something we are all born with and it's our internal healing mechanism that repairs our body. My own experience with healing started at a spiritual healing church as a young mother. Healing and meditation gradually became part of my life.

I noticed as people came for healing they just wanted to feel the touch. I discovered there are several levels of touch:

- Emotionally people just wanted to be loved and cared for and acknowledged.
- Mental level people wanted something to feel good about, like something they have achieved, contributed or developed.
- Spiritually is an identity many people need to have a connection to a deeper part of themselves.

Meditation started my day and brought a peace that always helped me stay positive. I went on to teach my method to my clients that helped them connect to the deeper part of themselves. It was easy to see how meditation and personal development play a significant role in connecting people to their inner truth or inner being that helps create harmony in their lives.

As I worked with men I noticed how healing and relationships are closely linked with sexual and intimate experiences. It all ties in with the energies at work within us, where a vast majority of men have issues with self-esteem and self worth and judge themselves on their own performance in the bedroom. I wanted to know what was behind the energy of attraction, sex and lovemaking. How does seduction relate to love, and to see love and sexual experience through spiritual eyes as union of spirits on a soul level.

My vision turned into a passion to open people up to the 'Zen' or higher part of themselves to elevate intimate relationships to a spiritual level and bring awareness to the treasures that lie within us all. When individuals access this level it progressively leads them to a stress free 'healthier life-style' creating more loving and balanced relationships and more caring productive human beings.

SYNOPSIS OF MY BOOK

Welcome to a wonderful new beginning and congratulations for taking the first step in going towards owning your own powerful energy your 'sexual energy' that leads you to an energized way of living.

It's like following a road map and discovering what might ordinarily seem hidden. Either you can guess at the general direction and get there eventually or follow a map and get there easily without the stresses involved. This book gives you a map to help get you to embrace your inner or higher self and connect that precious part of you to every part of your experiences to help you with your destination in your life.

The practical advice in these pages will provide you with a combination of:-

- Exercises and methods that enable you to develop your own inner resources and powerful tools.
- Provides you with the means to have control over your emotions in life's situations.
- Understand your relationships how to identify the positive in every part of them
- To identify and break through obstacles that stand in your way to your abilities.
- Discover how your own genius is linked to your internal energy source.

- How to use your positive energy in order to sustain youthfulness.
- How you can get your power back and how to plug into your energy and turn it on like a switch.
- Discover what your sexual energy truly is, how to use it to maintain feel good feelings at anytime.

There is a universal law that when you follow it everything becomes easy including having an energized new life. This law states: **"Whatever you focus on you draw to you."** This law applies to absolutely everything and applies to both ends of the scale, so if you are in fear that something could happen, you are unwittingly drawing it closer to you. Another way of saying whatever you focus on, expands.

Have you noticed when you are having a good time how the 'fun side of you' is present, then disappears when you are working or busy? When I finally discovered how this works I knew then that I could access this side of my personality at any given time, what an awakening to realize. So I didn't have to go seeking it from another person or give my energy away to others in search of fulfillment. We all seem to do this on an unconscious level and we do this with sex also and let go of that feel good feeling once the experience is over.

We seem to play this game with ourselves. Until we can become conscious and observe how we go about doing this, then we can move onto more fulfilling relationships and tap into the fun side of ourselves easily and experience the deeper level of feel good feelings at will.

This book is divided into chapters on how to access all of the above and take care of every part of your life. These methods and exercises are key to increasing your health, your pleasure in and out of the bedroom. The benefits are endless.

Prologue: Sexual Magic

Sex—a word with multiple meanings, manifestations, and images that expresses the most fundamental instinct of the animal kingdom. For us mortals, sexuality is the expression of how we experience ourselves as sexual beings biologically, physically, emotionally, and so on. This word, so popular that it is the most searched for on the Internet, can cover nearly all aspects of the human condition and embrace cultural, political, philosophical, and spiritual issues.

Regarding human sexuality, Leonardo Boccadoro and Sabina Carulli, in their articles on "Art and Science of Sexual Magic," state:

"Human sexuality is not simply imposed by instinct or stereotypical conducts, as it happens in animals, but it is influenced both by superior mental activity and by social, cultural, educational and normative characteristics of those places where the subjects grow up and their personality develops. Consequently, the analysis of sexual sphere must be based on the convergence of several lines of development such as affectivity, emotions and relations". Mind Powers - The Art and Science of Sexual Magic, by Damon Lacourious.

Sex has dictated the course of history materially and non-materially. It is a wonder of human existence that has yet to be fully unravelled. For many, it is the vehicle of procreation, whereas for others it is merely a source of pleasure. Some have been inspired by it to pursue and develop spiritual paths and exercises, to transcend themselves, and to partake in the 'other'. Its power has also been used as a dreadful weapon to destroy, humiliate, and enslave. Despite all its various uses, our relation to it is the one uniting feature of humanity we all accept and recognize. Even the absence of it is an affirmation of its existence.

What is peculiar to modern societies is not that they consign sex to a shadow existence but that they dedicate themselves to speaking of it ad infinitum while exploiting it "as a secret".

Although it is evident from recovered art and artefacts, human achievements, and monuments that sex has always been a central feature of our existence, never has it had such a powerful, ambiguous, and obsessive presence as it does today. Wherever one turns, one is confronted, seduced, aroused, and terrorized by it. Never has it been so available but also distant, like an elusively flirting spectre.

It is no wonder that sexuality has become intertwined with another fascinating, exciting, and terrifying feature of human existence that has yet to be understood and fully accepted—magic. It is as if two labyrinths of dark and light have become one.

A Short History of Sex Magic

Sexuality and the occult arts have long been in a state of unholy and tempting matrimony in the Western imagination. Since at least the days of the alleged gnostic heretical acts of worship, the continuing persecution of the Templars and the Cathars, and the witch frenzy of the Middle Ages, illicit sexual behaviour has been linked to acts of magic or what the accusers believed to be acts of magic.

Beyond the realm of ecclesiastical condemnations and misleading evocations of an ungodly, pagan past, sexuality has flourished in schools of Western esotericism, from the Jewish mystical kabbalah to the Renaissance magic of Marsilio Ficino. Born October 19, 1433, Figline, Republic of Florence, (Italy), Ficino was an Italian philosopher, theologian, and linguist whose translations and commentaries on the writings of Plato and other classical Greek authors generated the

Florentine Platonist Renaissance, which influenced European thought for two centuries. Giordano Bruno (original name Filippo Bruno, born 1548, near Naples) was an Italian philosopher, astronomer, mathematician, and occultist whose theories anticipated modern science. The most notable of these were his theories of the infinite universe and the multiplicity of worlds, which maintained a finite universe with a sphere of fixed stars.

The sexual mysticism of Emanuel Swedenborg arose during the Enlightenment. He was one of Europe's truly great minds, and we can attribute that to the success of his mission as a teacher and philosopher of the spirit.

All these examined how the physical union of male and female sexuality conjoined the active and passive aspects of the divine here on earth. But not until the middle of the nineteenth century did the relationship between esoteric beliefs and sexuality become a series of practices and attitudes and a specific category of magic.

Hugh B. Urban, in his exceptional book *Magia Sexualis: Sex, Magic, and Liberation in Western Esotericism*, clearly identifies the superficiality and ignorant approach contemporary Westerners have toward sexual magic. http://books.google.com.au/books/about/Magia_Sexualis.html?id=6wVBx9yriTUC&redir_esc=y

Judging by the proliferation of titles in bookstores and cyberspace, sexual magic is understood in simple terms by most American readers: it is most commonly defined as the "art of extended orgasm," or "peak experience in sexual loving."

According to Margo Anand, a widely read New Age author, sexual energy can be refined and expanded, transporting you to realms of orgasmic delight that offer an endless variety of exquisite experiences. This is a type of magic.

Why did sex magic flourish in the middle to the late nineteenth century and continue to this day? Despite many attempts on behalf of "authorities" to present sex magic as the purest expression of ancient Western esotericism and a well-kept occult secret that has reached us from the dawn of ages, this magical practice—like many of those who advocate it—is not a rejection of secular modernity but rather an affirmation of many of modernity's ideals.

These ideals reflect ideas such as progress, the affirmation of the individual as the ultimate force in the universe, the recognition of the multidimensional and powerful reality of sex, a scientific endeavour to unravel the secrets of the universe, and the overwhelming potential of free will as a form of liberation from suppressive institutions. This coincides with the endeavour to re-enchant a demystified and secularized modern industrial world through the occult.

I am not implying that sex magic lends itself to superficially relating to a glorified past of arcane knowledge and constant sacred communion with the divine; indeed, contemporary occultism has been effectively inspired by esoteric traditions of the past and has been reaffirmed, rediscovered, and reinterpreted in this age. It must be admired for its courage to seek out means to adapt esotericism to a disenchanted world of secular thought and scientific cynicism. Nor am I proclaiming that sex magic is merely a mask for movements of social change and that all ideas and practices revolving around sexual magical are romantic decorations of new, radical movements that aspire only to cultural liberation and social transformation.

It is my belief that for sex magicians such as Aleister Crowley in his book *Golden Dawn*, their sacred art and science is one fully preoccupied with a search for esoteric truths through their personal relationships with the absolute, magical universe they inhabit. It might be a combination of socio-cultural and supernatural effects that caused sex magic to transit into contemporary occultism. Emanuel Swedenborg (1688–1772), born in Stockholm, was renowned in his day for his respectable contributions to various fields of natural science. His writings, at first oriented toward anatomy, physiology, and psychology, gained quite a bit of recognition. Later in his life, however, he underwent a religious crisis and began to tell of purported experiences of having been in communication with spiritual entities from beyond. His later works abound with vivid descriptions of what life after death is like. Again, the correlation between what he wrote about some of his spiritual experiences and what those who have come back from close calls with death report is amazing.

Why has sex magic drawn so much attention? According to occultists, sex magic transcends the principles of hedonism and is in essence a powerful manifestation of magic aligned with cosmic forces and correspondences. The rationale is that if non-spiritual sex can create new life, intentional, ritualized forms of sexual intercourse can give birth to the greatest supernatural effects and results. As Aleister Crowley stated in his introduction to *Magia Sexualis,* "The root idea is that any form of procreation other than normal is likely to produce results of a magical character." Crowley practiced the dark arts, so his comments come from his experiences that were of a negative nature and frequently bizarre.

During the Victorian Era in America, the tremendous power of human sexuality was slowly recognized scientifically and socially, praised within the confines of marriage and condemned outside of it. It was also an era of radical social movements and of various new religious movements, especially the Spiritualist movement, all of which were concerned with the spiritual side of sexuality but not all in the same fashion.

Paschal Beverly Randolph, physician, philosopher, world traveller, Supreme Grand Master of the Fraternitas Rose Crucis, and member of

L'Ordre du Lis of France, the Double Eagle of Prussia, and Order of the Rose of England, was born in New York City on October 8, 1825. His main contribution to Western occultism concerned sex. Apart from being an expert in the cure of sexual diseases and dysfunctions, he claimed to have developed a system and practice of sexual magic that could achieve all manner of worldly and otherworldly marvels. He saw his system of sexual magic as a path to a millennial new world. Randolph's system of sexual magic was described by Hugh B. Urban as; "a system of magical eroticism, or affection alchemy." Randolph states in *Sex Magic and the Eleventh Wave,*

> Love lieth at the foundation…and Love is convertibly passion, enthusiasm affection heat, fire, SOUL, God… The nuptive moment, the instant wherein the germs of a possible new being are lodged… is the most solemn, serious, powerful and energetic moment he can ever know on earth.

Randolph believed the sexual drive was the most potent and fundamental force in the universe due to its natural attraction between the active/positive and the passive/negative. Following Franz Anton Mesmer's pattern of thought, Randolph understood the male and female as opposite yet complementary electromagnetic forces, with the male genitals being the positive and the female the negative.

Randolph states, "Because sexual attraction is the most potent and fundamental force in nature, the experience of orgasm is a very primordial, powerful and critical moment in human consciousness", from Mind Power News, New Dawn Magazine. It is the key to magical power. At the moment of climax, the soul is exposed to the energies of the universe and new life pours from the spiritual into the material realm. At this point, anything truly willed can happen.

A unique feature of his sexual techniques, apart from the employment and magical use of the orgasm as a means of acquiring otherworldly sympathies, was the mutuality and equality of male and female in their loving union. According to Randolph, all forms of sexual abuse in the Victorian framework, "whether through masturbation or excessive intercourse, drained the body of the vital energy required for the undertaking of a sexual magical operation."

Although he was accused by many of promoting promiscuity and sexual license under the guise of his sexual magical teachings, Randolph was indeed a very conservative character. His practice of sexual magic was anything but mere hedonistic license. Sex, for Randolph, was strictly for married couples in a state of pure love. Notes Randolph, in his *Sex Magic*,

> Free-love, disguise it as you may, means sensual license,
> no more, no less; and wherever its doctrine prevail there
> will you find either a worn-out debauchee, a freedom-
> shrieking woman of faded charms ... or brainy men,
> actually heartless un-emotive, spasmodically lecherous.

Although for many in nineteenth-century Victorian America Randolph might appear to be a radical spiritual antinomian (when Christians are released by grace from the obligation of observing the moral law) threatening the moral and spiritual foundation of society, his teachings on spiritualized love and sexual magic reflect and embody many of the basic sexual values of his day, physically and spiritually. His system was unlike any of the sexual techniques developed by the many magicians he inspired. His teachings could be no further from the sex "magick" of the notorious Aleister Crowley.

Sex Magik and the Great Beast

When one conjures up images and sensations of sexual magic, one generally stumbles upon Aleister Crowley before anyone else. Known in the press of his day as "the wickedest man in the world" and self-proclaimed "Great Beast 666," Crowley was the object of much scandal and moral outrage. Rejecting the prudence of Victorian society, Crowley saw sex magic as a supreme source of magical power. Unlike Randolph, Crowley did not confine sexual magic to the state of holy matrimony and made use of "outrageous" sexual acts, such as masturbation and homosexual intercourse, which shocked and horrified British society.

However, despite being the "sexual hedonistic deviant" and "the spawn of Satan," as portrayed by the popular press of the early twentieth century, Crowley had an important influence on Western occultism that should not be overlooked. By rejecting Victorian morality and identifying sex as the supreme magical source, he introduced new dimensions to the study and practice of the occult. His study of Buddhism and Hinduism transmitted new ideas and techniques that affected the Western esoteric tradition in a tremendous way. These ideas and many more have made him one of the most influential figures in the revival of magical traditions.

Born Edward Alexander Crowley in 1875, he was the son of a highly zealous and prudent father well established in the excessively puritanical Plymouth Brethren. He was raised in a strict Christian home in late Victorian England. In addition to teaching on the occult and sexual excess, Crowley was also a prolific poet and an avid mountain climber.

Despite taking delight in the accusations hurled at him, he was, according to Lawrence Sutin, one of his biographers, an enigmatic, gifted, and misunderstood character and "one of the rare human beings

... to dare to prophesy a distinctive new creed and to devote himself ... to the promotion of that creed" (*Unleashing the Beast*). He studied at the University of Cambridge and inherited a lot of money, which he spent travelling the world, publishing his works, and indulging in excess.

In 1904, Crowley received a revelation from an entity called Aiwass, which Crowley claimed was his guardian angel. Aiwass appeared and dictated to him the *"Liber al vel legis"- to verify voter identification* (*The Book of the Law*), which claimed that Crowley was to be the herald of the third aeon of humankind—the Aeon of Horus. His infamy as a black magician and "the wickedest man in the world" surfaced again in the 1920s, when he founded the Abbey of Thelema at a farmhouse in Cefalu, Sicily. In his autobiographical account, *Confessions*, he wrote,

> The shocking evils, which we all deplore around the question of sex, are principally due to the perversions produced by suppressions. The feeling that it is shameful and the sense of sin cause concealment ... that creates internal conflict and distortion, neurosis, and ends in explosion ... Each individual has an absolute right to satisfy his sexual instinct as is physiologically proper for him. (*Unleashing the Beast.*)

According to Crowley, the secret of sex magic is so tremendously powerful that

> if this secret which is a scientific secret were perfectly understood ... there would be nothing which the human imagination can conceive that not be realized in practice ... If it were desired to have an element of atomic weight six times that of uranium that element could be produced as 9. (*Unleashing the Beast.*)

Crowley did have some very good knowledge of Indian yoga and was aware of some of the key features and practices of Indian Tantra. Unlike most Orientalist scholars, he did not denounce Tantra but instead described it as a valid form of religion and the most advanced form of Hinduism. In his works, he frequently used the words *lingam* and *yoni*, tantric words for the male and female sexual organs. However, as N. N. Bhattacharyya has argued, most Western authors and magicians, Crowley included, misinterpret and misrepresent Tantra by approaching it only in terms of its sexual elements. Whereas Western magical systems have placed emphasis on the act of sex from the beginning, in traditional Hindu Tantra, sexual union is a minor part of the spiritual practices, and when it does take place, it is merely one method of awakening Shakti, the female principle of divine energy, especially when personified as the supreme deity Parvati.

Goddess Parvati is regarded as the power and divine consort of Lord Shiva - the Destroyer. Like her consort Shiva, Goddess Parvati is said to have both mild and terrible aspects, though generally she has a charming personality. Married women adore Parvati for her happy married life as she is usually pictured together with Lord Shiva, and their sons **Ganesha and Kartikeya** that depicts an ideal example of family unity and love.

Goddess Parvati is known by different names like Lalita, Uma, Gauri, Kali, Durga, Haimavati etc. Two of her fierce but very powerful forms are Durga (Goddess beyond reach) and Kali (Goddess of Destruction). As the mother of the universe, Parvati is known as Amba and Ambika, which means 'mother'. As Lalita, she represents the aspect of beauty.

Even Kenneth Grant, one of Crowley's most devoted students, admitted that Crowley's knowledge of Tantra was limited. Crowley conceived the rational mind as an act of departing and an irregularity of the true human self. He believed he discovered with his system of sex magic a way of destroying the rational mind at the point of orgasm and inducing a sense of natural trance and spiritual clarity not confined by the burden of the mundane and the rational. At this climaxing point, the divine is allowed to enter into the magical consciousness of the magician.

This is how a spiritual experience would be perceived when experimenting with mind and drugs, especially when a person has not connected with his or her internal power to experience transcendence, which takes the person beyond any system Crowley devised. The divine overtakes only when an individual is open enough and connects with this greater part of him or herself. Here Crowley talks about the divine being "allowed," as though one controls this power. On the other hand, the divine is an internal force that *is* and that we humans are expressions of, and until we become aware of it, we are unconscious of this internal power within us that we can connect with naturally.

He notes, "As man loses his personality in physical love, so does the magician annihilate his divine personality in that which is beyond. In love the individuality is slain ... Love destroyeth self ... Love breedeth All and None in One" (*The Book of Lies*).

Crowley believed that the purpose of sex magic beyond acquiring worldly things was to achieve supreme spiritual power and the power to conceive a divine child, a godlike being. Unlike Randolph, however, within this magical operation, the woman, whom Crowley regarded as inferior and limited, was merely a passive vehicle for the male magician to use in his sexual magical rites.

Individuality is not slain, as Crowley points out; it is merely transcended. You literally step out of it into another realm as you would step out of water onto land. This is the reason Crowley saw woman as inferior and a passive vehicle for male magicians.

In my view, based on my experience of practising and teaching meditation, this clearly shows Crowley had no concept of the divine self or power that resides and is unconscious within all people naturally and has nothing to do with gender.

The Bedchamber of Sex Magic

Modern sex magic has been associated with some very enigmatic, remarkable, and sometimes radical personalities. Randolph and Crowley have been most closely associated with sexual magic and have influenced generations of magicians with their pioneering visions. In the popular imagination, Randolph and Crowley came to represent an outcry for liberation from the suffocating pressures of the Victorians. This is evident from Randolph's system of sex magic, a path to the dawn of a new era in which the inequalities of Victorian America could not exist as the innermost secrets of human life surfaced. Although at first glance Crowley's vision appears not to share some of these desires and hopes, upon further scrutiny it becomes apparent that Crowley too was a remarkable reflection of his era, and he was indeed struggling against what he conceived as hypocritical and fallacious.

John Symonds met Aleister Crowley in 1946, the year before Crowley's death. Crowley's will left the copyrights for his works to Symonds and made him Crowley's literary executor, although Crowley's legal status as an undischarged bankrupt meant the copyrights ended up in receivership. At first fascinated by Crowley, Symonds became increasingly critical of his ideas and manners, in particular the use of drugs and free sex.

With Kenneth Grant, Symonds edited Crowley's autobiography and a number of other works. He authored four biographical works of his own: *The Great Beast* (1952), *The Magic of Aleister Crowley* (1958), *The King of the Shadow Realm* (1989), and *The Beast 666* (1997).

According to Symonds, Crowley was a contemporary of Freud; he grew out of the matrix of Victorianism … He was one of many who helped to tear down the false, hypocritical, self- righteous attitudes of the time. What is peculiar in Crowley's case is not that he chose evil but that in his revolt against his parents and God he set himself up in God's place. (*Unleashing the Beast.*)

It is with this background that these two sex magicians, Randolph and Crowley, ultimately came as explorers of the ambivalent tension between romantic and sexual love, the place of non-reproductive sexual acts, the importation of and experimentation with exotic sexual techniques from the "Orient," and so on. They have come to reflect many of the themes and paradoxes of modernity such as striving for individualism, a utopian future, the exploration of the meaning of sexuality, and our essence.

Crowley conceived the art and science of sex magic to be one of the most powerful occult systems. Many esotericists have expressed the view that the human mind is the gateway of magic through which the magician gains access to the astral plane and through which the magical universe works. For some magicians, the basic structure of the psyche consists of the conscious mind, also known as the waking consciousness, and the subconscious, also known as the unconscious, the realm of our being experienced in dreams and altered states of consciousness. There is also a kind of "censor" that separates these two parts of the psyche and acts as a filter, ensuring the selective gathering of empirical perception and the protection of the conscious mind from uncontrolled flooding from the subconscious. Magic makes use of both the "rational" and the "irrational" parts of the psyche.

In some cases, this censor is either missing altogether as happens with people who have been diagnosed with schizophrenia, or it acts as a gateway through which psychics can gain access into the "other" realm. This realm is part of the unconscious mind where huge potential lies; this is what was explored by Crowley where he took great risks to venture and tempt the forces hidden in that world unseen by us. When people have no knowledge that these forces can be controlled, the forces are likely to overtake them. If only the diagnosed patients were given the opportunity to discover that they have within their power a "switch" they can open and close at will. **Instead, they are medicated and labelled**.

The key element in every magical operation is introducing this understanding of the psyche to the magical formula of combining will and imagination, which in turn affects the psyche. The key result can be referred to as a "magical trance," the very peak of a ritual ecstasy in which the cosmic forces are invoked and manifested. For sex magicians, the best way to achieve this altered state of consciousness, this magical trance, this death-like feeling of emptiness when the magician becomes the vessel for magical forces, is the orgasm. It could be seen this way by those without a spiritual connection with their higher parts, as expressed in Crowley's system of magic.

Beyond the social analysis, psychological enquiry, and historical investigation, the true inspiration for these two magicians and others who came later was the search for an ultimate magical system based on occult correspondences and a deeper understanding of the mechanisms of the self or by making sex a way of communing with the magical universe and the pure, whirling forces that inhabit it.

Their efforts were more than just an outcry for liberation or a struggle against oppressive taboos; for them it was a magical attempt to enchant a disenchanted world. The path that could lead them into a state of union with the divine is a method to acquire supreme spiritual powers that could affect both the natural and the supernatural. The expression of their will and imagination enabled us to explore our sexuality and become more open with it. Tantra would eventually become more accepted, even if it were more popular in yoga classes, which slowly took over the Tantra practices worldwide.

Our Divine Selves

We are all born with "central intelligence," or the God source that resides within us all as love. Because of this, our sole purpose is to recognize and live out of love more fully. We become more human this way. This is what the ancient texts such as the Vedas and Upanishads refer to as "the way the truth and the light," also in the Bible.

Only in this way can we live by "the laws of god," living in harmony with the totality of ourselves. This harmony is the law of balance. When we find balance on all levels, within ourselves we want for nothing more, as only in this way can we live in harmony with others and ourselves and share it with everyone. This law of harmony and balance promotes personal health, longevity, and an internal youthfulness often reflected in the physical body. When we live within these laws, our lives become examples to others as this harmony is felt by others, and they inspire others to strive for this peace and truth, bringing abundance on a personal and planetary level.

By acknowledging the divinity in one another, we evoke that presence in ourselves, which is at the heart of all relationships, and at a deeper level, it is where lovers are equal opposites of each other.

Preface

I always knew no matter what challenging life situations I faced, I could always go inward and come out feeling refreshed. Using this strategy, I've found a way of maintaining a happy, balanced life. I call it *applying the laws of life*, and it has helped me stay connected to loving feelings and in control in the face of so many of life's challenges. This life recipe helped me maintain my youthful body and stay energized by keeping a balanced lifestyle. Following these laws, I was able to create a set of essential life skills contributing to a successful and balanced life on all levels.

I now live in a lush part of Sydney with bay views and just a five-minute walk to a beautiful beach where, I still I do handstands, swim, scuba dive, and dance. I live a very happy, exciting life, and for the last few years I've been teaching men how to connect to their hearts and feelings, which enhances their self- esteem and also their sexual performance and relationships in general. This has helped men realize that to have a happy relationship or successful marriage they need to connect to their feelings rather than their genitals. When men disconnect from their hearts, especially in business, they resort to genital relief to release stress, which may be nice in the short term but is never really satisfying in the long term.

I included references in the prologue to sexual origins from the early twentieth century to throw light on how disconnections due to vital energy being drained from the body due to excess of sex or masturbation have been perpetuated and how this information has always been there. By opening yourself to awareness of how you can have extended sexual pleasure and enjoyment, you can do so without draining your energy in the process.

I hope this book helps men have healthier and more enjoyable sex lives free of performance issues or guilt that arises from lack of self-esteem. It explains why women will find it in their best interests to sexually please their men more frequently, preventing them from seeking relief elsewhere, a very common issue.

Readers will discover how we camouflage our innermost needs and how our needs contribute to relating to the opposite sex. When we change our perspective on our needs, we can turn matters around from being driven by them to the fun part of being together. It brings me joy to know I'm creating more understanding in many troubled relationships and changing the perception in this fast technological world with its emphasis on doing and achieving, which has caused us to forget to spend time on feeling and connecting. Only by linking up to our own feel-good feelings, sharing, and spreading this naturally and easily can we experience and connect to our hearts.

Connecting with their hearts enables men to connect to the women in their lives and build more- permanent connections to love and happiness generally rather than chasing the missing feelings that slowly empty their souls through gambling, adult services, and pornography.

Statistics show that a minimum of 20,000 men per year in America have triple bypass surgery; due to stress related factors rather than cholesterol. Many more men don't make it to the operating table, and this figure does not include quadruple or double bypass surgery recipients.

Introduction

Orgasmic Effect (Abbreviated): Orgasmic—Rhythm—Generating—Active—Sensation—**on a Microcosmic level**—Effectively. This actually describes your healing energy that flows through your body, and the more aware you are of your own energy, the more your expanded energy is then felt by others.

I worked as a counsellor and therapist most of my life, and although I was always attending seminars and eventually became a life coach so I could help my clients solve their issues faster, I noticed that people resisted addressing their problems and postponed not only their appointments but also taking responsibility for their problems.

When a health situation arose for me, I had to put my life on pause for a year. This gave me time to discover a new way of working, using massage. I was living very close to the city of Sydney, so I thought I could give it a try until I got back on my feet. It always surprises me how "the universe" comes to your aid when you are open to the answer **of** the **"what's next"** question, as though putting what you need in your lap.

I didn't expect clients to start arriving as quickly as they did, and I was amazed at how quickly they just wanted to lie down, relax, and be massaged.

In the past, I'd always made clients feel better with relaxation based on getting them in touch with their bodies, using the breath for releasing stress. This was part of my therapy when I did regression and stress-related counselling with males and females alike. I found myself slowly incorporating my previous techniques of relaxation and visualization into the massage sessions for men I started to pay attention to the messages I received and how those various methods could enhance the experience for my clients. My training as a healer and life coach kicked in, and I began to pick up on energy running through people. I was being instructed as though from within, and I gradually connected with energy meridians and the chakra system as I worked with my clients.

I noticed how so many men came in secret and had guilt issues about their partners not knowing they were getting sensual massages. It slowly came to my attention that a great number of males were having a problem with premature ejaculation and under-performance associated with lack of self-esteem and guilt issues. I didn't put this together, until I began observing males and listening to the issues they'd bring up along with their questions. While I was gathering this information purely from what males were telling me about themselves, I began to realize I was collecting valuable data, the type collected in research material. Yet instead of having to actively gather this data, it came walking through my front door and just presented itself to me unasked.

In order to understand the process we want to know in any situation, we need to go into its very core in order to get the answers. As in the British TV series "The Silent Witness" where the woman pathologist, played by the actress Amanda Burton – had to examine gruesome corpses in order to identify the causes and circumstances surrounding their demise.

In the same way I too had to go into the depths of personal human experiences and touch the physical parts of the male anatomy in order to unlock all the understanding behind how our energy moves. What blocks our energy and why we do what we do? Why it becomes necessary to go to some of the extremes that males go to for gratification, and how these behaviors are copied as a general rule by others; how its all passed on down through the generations, simply because the understanding of higher consciousness that is connected with energy, is not generally explored let alone practiced.

I gradually developed a method of bringing the energy through their bodies, getting them to focus on the energy itself, and guiding them through a visualization during which I'd bring to their minds a particularly delightful experience and connect it with the sensual massage they were receiving.

Guys would frequently tell me how girls were usually "switched off," which caused them to feel the same way. No wonder they kept trying to find girls who would give them the feel-good feeling without switching off and spending large sums of money all in the name of feeling good and feeling relaxed through touch.

I began informing men what switching off did to them in the long run and how the women who performed full-service massage also had to be switched off. Surprisingly, many men wholeheartedly agreed and recognized this as true. So began my quest to bring to men what they were missing: 'connection'. It was from these beginnings that my techniques evolved.

Based on what all the men were sharing with me, I began to realize that the missing factor every time with males, was simply they were disconnected-firstly from themselves. As a result of this disconnection, those whose relationships were based mostly on their performance in the bedroom found that their performance would suffer along with their work performance, and I noticed a common thread: males seemed to judge themselves and make their bedroom performance their primary comparison.

I also noticed that many men who came to learn the techniques frequently were without partners. What was missing? Some males had broken up with partners, or had never had partners, or were 'too old' for one. Some were millionaires who could perform quite well in the bedroom.

By establishing connections with themselves, males began to feel improved connection with their relationships and the world around them. I coined the phrase *"the orgasmic effect,"* which describes inner connection that the practice of the techniques enables males to connect with their own orgasmic energy. The techniques also give them the additional lasting power that all males seem to seek separately.

The more I refined my techniques, the easier men got the connection with themselves and the lasting power the techniques gave them. None of the extra long-term health benefits that the techniques bring seemed to be as important to them as being able to last longer in the bedroom. I always held out for the possibility of an advanced male who might see the deeper connections the techniques gave as the more important factor.

On occasion I'd come across the rare male who wanted to go to the next level rather than stay just with the sexual, but even he was generally not keen to explore this connection further if it didn't involve more sexual content. I discovered, however, that when men knew about our energy centres or chakras, they had a deeper understanding of the spiritual reality that connected sex with the rest of the body. These aware males recognized how internal balance includes a healthy lifestyle, including releasing personal issues, which is all part of the overall fitness of the internal energy system. Men are generally not willing to look inward, and only very few of them are aware enough to go to that next level.

As I took males through the program, many things opened my eyes to how men go about releasing their pent-up stress. It was nothing like how women released their stress, which I learnt from males informing me about it through the jokes, questions, and references they'd make about their appetites. I was all the while collecting valuable information and data on the behaviour and how males think in general.

I now had a full program for informing men about their general patterns for stress relief and opening them up to an easier and far less costly way of bringing more harmony to the home and their relationships in general. In addition, my method had facets that can improve a man's general well being and reduce heart and prostate problems as a result of his being in control of his energy. Lasting longer in the bedroom became the bonus.

Chapter 1

Mens' Secrets

Working with males on releasing stress gave me the idea to write down their responses and get valuable feedback away from any intrusive cameras and without their partners knowing what they did to release stress. It became like a survey I collected responses to in a private setting. I hope the information below will also serve as valuable to females by providing insight on what they generally have no idea about males secret lives.

Why Men are Attracted to Women

Though men think they are after women's sexual prowess, which is what men are initially attracted to, it is their warmth and nurturing that gives women the healer quality that men generally lack and which they subconsciously seek from their women.

Men's strong, dominant, linear aspect gives them the assertive streak that does not give them easy access to relaxation, and this is where women come in. Women's natural predisposition to the lateral side of their nature opens them up to relaxation part of their nature. This dominance factor is exactly why, when working closely with men, women tend to take on men's assertive streak. Consequently, they too succumb to the response this role carries and may also seek similar types of release. These women will seek the sexual rather than relaxation-type releases by going to alternative adult services provided by male masseuses with extras.

Because women are more laterally minded, they are more open to the opinions and views of others even though they may be biased. Because women generally have this capacity, they tend to spread their views around among themselves and others. This makes women chatty and fun, and this is what men are attracted to.

It is not practical for a man to have sex each time he needs to release some sexual tension, and the sexual jokes males constantly indulge in reflect this constant tension. However, a man does need to release tension, and releasing it gives him balance, providing him with a happier, more stress-free working life.

When we examine how responsibility affects stress, we see that stress builds up as tension in the head. To balance the energy in the body, men need to go to the opposite end of their anatomy to release this stress. Generally, when I have asked men "What exists between the head and the genitals?" the answer is usually something like, "Ummm, blood," or "I've never thought about that." They search the ceiling for an answer and eventually say, "The stomach." It appears, therefore, that men don't seem to connect with this part of their anatomy.

If a hundred women were asked that question, most would answer, "The heart." If men connected with their hearts more, they would not only be far better lovers but would also have a greater sense of peace and connectedness. When a man connects with himself on the inside, he is not only more relaxed but also happier and more at ease, and his world is more available to him on many more levels.

Men need the love, the nurturing, and the softness that comes from women, yet they "think" this feeling is sexual, and they're therefore attracted sexually. This is because men are internally programmed for procreation. To them, nurture subconsciously translates as sexual. This stimulates their competitive natures and drives them to want to achieve and find partners to procreate with.

When men have more testosterone, as do fighters and boxers, the type of females they are likely to choose will be their extreme opposite. Hence, she will more likely be the defenceless, helpless type with few assertive qualities, one who looks for a more powerful, muscular male to rely on for everything. This stimulates the male to continue building muscle. This can easily be observed with many couples.

For the man who has developed more of his "feminine" side, the need for defence drops off considerably, and he feels more comfortable with this side of his nature, which gives him more balance. A male's sexual release provides some "tangible balance" that he needs, which releases the urgency to constantly chase the opposite sex to bring him a temporary relaxed feeling.

We generally seek balance and search for this outside ourselves. Internal balance is something we all strive to find to fill that void, hence the expressions, "It just feels like there is something missing" or "I just don't feel satisfied no matter how I throw myself into my work." Men can now have access to this previously elusive balance by using a simple method I have developed of simple techniques that reduce their tiredness, stress, and anxiety and additionally bring a lighter, more alive, and happier feeling into their bodies. It is nice to hear this general response from males who have learnt and continue practicing this method.

To conclude: Men need love and nurture even though they may connect this with sexual attraction. The more balanced males are, the happier they will be within and won't feel there is something missing, as is the general case when males are out of balance with themselves.

General Understanding of Sexual Energy

We generally understand sexual energy as an emotional tension usually followed by a pleasant euphoric sensation when released. Imagine allowing this energy to spread throughout your body and absorbing this very energy through all your cells. Now imagine this to be a switch that allowed you to turn on additional energy whenever you were feeling down, without sex. You will read in these pages how to find this method, which not only gives you this ability but can also unblock the energy within you, which is the energy drain that predisposes males to premature ejaculation and not lasting very long in the bedroom, frustrating their partners.

Sexual energy is an emotion that can be activated, as can be gratitude, love, appreciation, and acknowledgement. We all know how important these emotions are and how we crave them. But we can't always get these higher, tender emotions in relationships, so it's natural to go for the most commonly obtainable emotion we can get, sex, even if its sex with no feelings involved.

Recent research has shown that when the coccyx is stimulated in women who have never been able to orgasm, they easily begin to do so and enjoy heightened sexual pleasure in a natural way. Women can now reclaim this energy also by simply connecting to and using this simple means and enjoying what they previously could not, getting a heightened connection and pleasure they never thought possible.

The Default Programming within the Male

During the years that I have worked with males, I noticed how many men didn't know that genital sensitivity was giving them below-average sexual enjoyment and how many didn't know it could be easily and naturally overcome. I soon realized this was one of the issues I needed to address.

It appears that there is no one to inform boys about their sexual health, and if their fathers are the only ones who could tell them but didn't know these things themselves, how can they grow into men knowing any differently? If most men don't realize that sensitivity of the foreskin is due to insufficient hygiene, they accept their acute sensitivity as normal and are not likely to visit a doctor who can inform them and correct this common problem. Most men "put up" with this sensitivity and decide it's connected with ejaculation. I have addressed this problem in full a little later on.

The way a man thinks is completely different from the way a woman thinks. This major difference between the genders reflects their differing needs. When these needs are unacknowledged, even though one may love another, there will always be a price to pay, and sometimes the damage can be insurmountable when these individual needs go unaddressed.

I've outlined here how the two sides can be much more compatible when they understand the other's *true needs*. Relationships end mostly due to the same problem: not because of sexual incompatibility but sexual miscommunication. This seems to be the truth most of the time, as the statistics show.

Males throughout all time and history have typically been the providers who carry most of the responsibility. As providers, males have an inbuilt need to provide, produce results, achieve, and succeed. Most of this is driven by their need to provide for their families and to produce results for work, and testosterone is what drives them to compete with one another to achieve. This is basically how males are subconsciously programmed.

The result of all this competition in the workplace that drives men to succeed and provide for their families carries considerable stress. Men will work even in dangerous situations; construction, mining, oil drilling, and so on, to succeed. Equal rights aside, very few females are physically capable of handling these jobs; in addition, males are able to perform these tasks without filtering them through their emotions.

Generally speaking, when a man is focused on a task, he is oriented in his head, where decisions are made, and he generally takes his decision seriously once he's made it. This is mainly because men generally do not share their decisions with other men. Women will consult their girlfriends or siblings before making decisions, which *releases* much of the stress that comes with decision-making. Men need to prove themselves as capable; hence their decisions are more personal and involve more stress than the decisions made by women. As a result, of accumulated stress by way of tension in their heads men have always known that the quickest way to release their built-up tension is through their genitals, and most men will do that through adult services. Many males also develop gambling or sexual or pornography addictions. If this were not a common trend with males, these would not be multibillion-dollar industries that they are the world over.

Ways Females Release Their Tension

Because women don't release their stress the way men do (i.e. releasing their tensions by going to adult services,) they generally don't think that men resort to adult services. They know such services exist, but they are generally in denial that their own man could possibly be among all the rest. Women usually accompany males and customarily prefer to sit at poker machines at clubs, but casinos and pubs are generally a man's domain. To discover this answer, you only need to observe the multiple beauty treatments that women visit to release their stress. Pubs and casinos are not places where women will sit around for a long time as men do.

The first thing women do when they meet one another is compliment each other: "I like your hair", "where did you get your shoes?" "I like your dress." They do not necessarily mean these compliments, but just as men are the providers who carry responsibility, women have always been the nurturers and healers. They will exchange compliments, catch up over coffees, and solicit each other's opinions on what they buy.

What happens generally with women is when they exchange opinions they're actually exchanging "feel- good feelings" in the process. Be that about the jeans or the handbag they bought or any other small cute item. It's the nature of women to share; hence, when they're feeling stressed, shopping for accessories uplifts their emotions, as women automatically process everything through their emotions. Women therefore are more likely to become shopaholics than are males.

Here's another example how feel-good feelings work for a woman: when moving into a new place, home, or flat with her man, the woman will generally be the one who purchases the cushions, rugs, bedspreads, pillow slips, and curtains. When her man comes home, she asks, "How do you like the bedspread (or new rug or curtains) honey?" He will glance at it and respond, "Yeah, good," with no additional emotion. Hence, women think that men do not appreciate them, but this is not the case; it's just a man's way of expressing this sort of thing, as a man sees the world from a rational rather than an emotional perspective.

A man, on the other hand, who enters a new dwelling will look over what needs to be done and will prioritize the tasks because that's the way he's oriented. This is the reason he doesn't like to be badgered by the woman, who may see things differently about when he "should" tackle any one task. She wants the jobs done as they fit in with her ideas of "setting the atmosphere." She connects with her emotions to everything she does but forgets that her man does not. It would serve women well to pay closer attention to this simple interaction with their man.

How Feel-Good Feelings Run Our Lives

Holidays demand a lot of planning; schedules, pets, garden, house sitting, finances, etc. When you come back from a holiday, you feel great for a while. As you settle back into everyday routine, you say you've come back to reality. Actually, reality is the great feeling you experience during the holiday, where you get to connect with the real you and all the good feelings that result from feeling free of the general obligations. This is the reason people hike, camp, parachute jump, hang glide ski, and scuba dive. A common way to feel free is to engage in activities such as these that give you the emotional release. Because men have a high level of testosterone, they need to release higher levels of emotional tension than women do.

So a few weeks after people return from holidays, they generally go back to the feeling of mediocrity and the doldrums. Most people don't realize they've let go of the good feelings, nor do they realize they don't know how to maintain that feel-good energy or how to keep positive feelings alive even if they wanted to.

Women will repeatedly share their experiences with their friends with pictures and stories, but we rarely see men doing so amongst each other. They will comment on their holidays but will not go into as much detail as do women; women like to process by going into their emotional experiences of their holiday, whereas men generally avoid sharing experiences unless it's with close friends. Without this openness, men struggle to hold things together, and when stress builds up, they struggle to unload it. Back from a holiday, a male still needs to find ways to continue releasing his stress and get some feel good feelings happening, for the next year or two before his next holiday or break.

To Conclude: As most men need to release stress frequently, they automatically connect this with sexual release in most cases. Additionally, they will reach out into the world using four easy avenues:- pubs, casinos, adult services, and pornography, that generally become very addictive ways for men to release stress, though these are seemingly the easiest means available to them.

Why Women Have Orgasms and Males Climax

Males have never stopped to wonder why they have strong urges to watch pornography. The reason is simple. When a female orgasms, her energy rises slowly up through her body. The higher the notes of the orgasmic "song" she sounds, the higher her energy has risen up her body via 'the chakras'. An orgasm leaves her feeling enlivened, and the orgasmic feeling may last for at least an hour afterward for a vast majority of women, leaving her feeling relaxed and energized. Many women will agree with this, and men who have observed this in women know this very well.

Males agree that instead of this feeling lasting them for an hour or two, they're lucky if the feeling lasts a few minutes. This is because men generally have a genital climax, not an orgasm, so the energy doesn't have a chance to flow through their bodies. When men ejaculate, they push their energy down, and many struggle even to ejaculate. Consequently, most men feel quite drained after genital climaxes. This is what every male I have interviewed and observed in my research has related. This is also the major reason men watch pornography—they love to see how women orgasm, and how that orgasm for women goes on and on with the clear visual expression on her face that expresses her enjoyment. However, how often do you hear of a woman wanting to watch how men ejaculate on the Internet? There's your answer for men's fascination with pornography, rather than women.

When a man ejaculates, it's simply the way his body is programmed for procreation, and he automatically assumes that ejaculating more frequently makes him a better stud; they judge their prowess by the number of times they ejaculate in one day, but the opposite is true. A man does not procreate every time he ejaculates; and what males do not realise is that they're just wasting their precious energy in the process, as noted in Paschal Beverly Randolph writings in the prologue. This is the reason males need sex frequently, unlike their female counterparts, who are satisfied by their orgasms. In fact, a man feels good just before and at the moment of ejaculation; as soon as he "comes," the nice feeling has gone, so he wants to feel it again with his woman. She, however, doesn't require sex so soon after but will usually agree because she may have experienced a multiple orgasm and wants that ecstatic feeling to continue.

Harnessing a Male's Precious Energy Increases His Performance and Health

This precious energy can be harnessed by men, by moving it through their bodies just as easily as women do when they have orgasms. Harnessing their energy leaves men feeling lighter, more alive, and refreshed, and all men can experience this. When men learn how to have this powerful energy flow through their bodies instead of constantly wasting it, they are also less likely to develop prostate or heart problems.

The reason for this is simple. When the male learns to get his energy to flow through his body, it also "recharges his batteries," leaving him feeling more alive and energised, which is precisely the feeling we get after a lovely walk in the forest or on the beach. The feeling of being energised after a walk in nature is not something that can be measured, but we all know this feeling well and can relate how such a walk can relax and refresh us. This simple and most natural way that leaves us feeling recharged and gives us long-term benefits needs no scientific "proof."

The technique described in these pages, gets his energy to flow through the body giving it the same recharging effect and additionally unblocks the build up of his energy when his sexual tension is not released through his genitals. Consequently, as a man gets older, sexual opportunities can be fewer because of financial or relationship responsibilities, or worse. He may feel he is not as attractive to females as he was before, which lessens his opportunity for sexual release. Sadly, his stress and tensions do not decrease.

As tension builds up with nowhere to go, the built-up sexual energy that was 'used to' being released, now starts choking up the avenue through which it was customarily released, and slowly accumulates creating prostate problems or heart problems, according to the way the man holds onto his tension. Men frequently refer to getting their "rocks" off, but no rocks are involved here—just accumulated energy. Women never use this expression, as their energy flows through their bodies with all the sharing and processing they do with emotional energy that men simply do not. Men generally agree they feel drained after sex, so it's easy to see how this common expression came to describe their energy without them even realizing it.

Here are some examples of how this works

- When a male has been holding onto suppressed anger or resentment for many years, his liver will begin to play up. Dr. Deepak Chopra writes about this in his book 'Perfect Health'. http://www.chopra.com/phtt-new#
- When he has been feeling disempowered (possibly due to finances) and or unappreciated for a long time, the dejected feeling of defeat weighs heavily on his heart, creating problems. See Louise Hay's 'You Can Heal Your Life' http://www.hayhouse.com.au/details.php?id=2901

- Holding onto unreleased tension that has nowhere to go, especially after his forties with additional ongoing competition, in which a male needs to prove himself; will slowly lead to prostate problems. See Louise Hay's '*You Can Heal Your Life*'.

The Energy Benefits—If Only Males Knew

Men can use this energy by dispersing it through their bodies and benefiting from it, just as a person who does yoga, breathing exercises, or meditation. When doing yoga or meditation you don't analyse in the middle of a class, but rather this is a time when the body and mind has a chance to relax and allow internal harmonizing and rebalancing to take place. Unfortunately, men don't do yoga in the numbers women do, nor do they give one another hugs, which is a custom among women in all countries.

When men stop hugging their sons and daughters (possibly when their children approach their teens), they are more likely to develop these issues because their hearts are not regularly as involved as they are with women. A survey needs to be done on this factor alone!

To Conclude: When men learn that "getting their rocks off" is actually the release of accumulated and blocked energy, they can learn an easy way to spread their precious energy throughout their bodies. As this energy flows more easily in their bodies with relaxed exercises, they could enjoy greater orgasms and become happier and healthier.

How Men Connect with Women

When a male looks at an attractive female, the first response he feels is in his genitals—that's just the way males are constructed so he naturally thinks what he *needs* from a woman is a sexual connection.

But if that were his main need, no male would contemplate a long-term relationship or marriage. It's a given that males *want* the sexual, but what do they *need?* The main part of what males need from females is nurturing. Without the nurturing factor, males find it difficult to deal with stress. When stress builds up for a man, he needs to release this stress, and without a woman,_releasing built-up tension through the genitals alone provides only temporary relief hence the ongoing search for sex.

Generally being the providers, carrying responsibilities, striving to produce results, and having to meet deadlines causes a male's tensions to rise. It's the nurturing factor from the female that provides him with the relief and the balance he needs.

Males have not concluded that the heart connection is the missing link that they really need, to achieve this balance in their lives.

What Does Genital Stress Release Do for a Man?

If we were to ask what releasing stress this way actually does for a man, he would answer, "It feels good for five minutes, but initially I feel drained of energy." In the days of old, when leaders led warriors into battle, they discouraged their warriors from sleeping with their wives the night before because it would drain their energy. This is told in the Biblical story of Sampson and Delilah. It wasn't because she cut his hair that he lost his strength; it was that she seduced him. Men know masturbation feels good while they fantasise about sex during the process, which is the reason for their interest in "dirty" pictures.

After such visualization, fantasising, and ejaculation, their energy exits via their genitals, causing them to feel drained, hence the fascination of watching women orgasm via pornographic sites it's the energy women exude during orgasm. For this reason, women are not inclined to watch other women orgasm nor watch males climax, as women are satisfied through their bodies with their orgasms rather than the genital climaxes men experience.

Women generally feel alive and energized and even give the appearance of glowing after good orgasms, and women usually look a lot younger when they have good sex partners or lovers. Scientists could learn much by measuring human energy and how the body lights up the aura into multicolour's that race through the cells when a woman orgasms.

There are special machines that can measure the human energy field, one study measured the energy in the hands when a person was doing a "healing." A machine that was developed in the 1930s for 'Kirilian photography' clearly shows the auric fields even around plants. http://en.wikipedia.org/wiki/Kirlian_photography Konstantin Korotkov. Another pioneer from Russia in the '60s, developed this further when he photographed energy surrounding our bodies and the energy displayed within our energy centres or chakras. Barbara Brennan, PhD, also shows these same colours in her book *Hands of Light*, http://www.barbarabrennan.com/ endorsed by Louise Hay and Elizabeth Kubler Ross; it's a must-read.

When Sexual Energy Does Not Reach the Heart

Sexual energy is an emotion. While the male is engaged with responsibilities, work, and family, he copes relatively well with releasing his pent-up emotional energy via his genitals. However, as he gets older, sexual frustrations mount due to growing family/work tensions, when his partner's libido may be reduced, especially when children are growing.

The male's preoccupation with business and providing for his family gradually leads to a loss of personal connection with his partner. If you stop dancing or stop riding a motorbike for a long while or stop using complex computer skills, your prowess in these activities will reduce. This applies to relationships as well, except that both males and females forget this very important principle.

In church groups, close communities establish a bond, and people feel connected to others through these very important links, or mechanisms. When men lose bonding with their partners and 'go astray', it's not because they are irresponsible or cannot be trusted; it's generally because they have lost the all- important connection with their partners, which causes them to lose connection with themselves, and the other way around. As this accumulated stress builds up it can cause aggressive behaviour and/or have negative effects on a male's health.

The All-Important 'Missing Factor'

The "something missing" in any person's life is all about loss of connection with oneself! People search for this lost connection sometimes by going through several relationships or spending time travelling, as young people do before settling down.

Relationships are all about connection, and this is why people love weddings; they are promises of wonderful support and connection, which is really love. All of us feel this love within ourselves, and this is why people stop whenever they see a wedding couple—the connection between the two is very tangible. We all want this connection, which is why relationships are the most popular subject in news and movies worldwide.

Women will talk with their girlfriends mostly about who met whom and what happened, while men talk about 'how far' they went, as portrayed in the movie *Grease*. (Listen in on any men's conversation at building sites.) Then, whenever there's a split up, women are generally sorry for their friend, because the hunt for the next person with whom she can establish a happy bond is on again sooner or later. This part is usually the talking point for women, who will actively give advice even to a total stranger about this common problem.

It's very hard on a man when he suffers a relationship breakup. Females go to their girlfriends for sympathy and advice, but men don't do this because they don't connect on an emotional level with other men. They don't relate to their friends by suggesting what other males should do. They try to hide their feelings with "She'll be right, mate," common Australian slang for "Forget about it," or "I'll shout you a drink" or "Let's go to the pub." Hence, the only way men generally know how to deal with their emotions is suppressing stress and tension by dismissing it and covering it up. Generally, a lot of this is "sorted" at a pub after a few drinks the stress has subsided, and by then no one is going to talk about personal issues.

This also leads to males becoming disheartened with relationships and going to adult services for a 'quick fix'. This further disconnects males from their feelings, and the more they withdraw, the more it will eventually affect their health. If a man has lost connection with a relationship, he will have disconnected from his feelings as a result, although chances are he disconnected from his feelings long before he lost the relationship. It was likely because he had been absorbed in his work or family stresses on both sides and gradually disconnected from his relationship over time. This slow disconnection from himself over time results in the 'something is missing feeling', that he tries to substitute in his life, that ends up being the factor leading to discord or health issues later on.

Male Prostate Issues vs. Women's Heart Connections

Because of this disconnection, a man's stress levels build up more and more. He attributes this to his work or responsibilities, but it is happening on the inside. As pressure builds, and he may not have the opportunity to release this pressure, it can put a strain on his heart, but he doesn't know that this may not show up on his tests initially if he actually gets them done.

Suppressed emotional energy builds up as stress and tension throughout the body. Every male is familiar with this uncomfortable feeling. When a man is depending solely on sexual release, he does not realize his energy is not flowing but exacerbating his tension because it's not being distributed throughout his body.

Although this may sound like a generalization, not releasing this pent-up tension has direct effects on the body, because everything that happens in the body is a direct result of how we manage our emotions, 'energy in motion'!

I cannot stress enough how connection with ourselves allows the 'feel-good feelings' to play an important role in many areas of our lives. Women deal with stress a lot more easily by buying little items. The energy spreads through their bodies, allowing them to feel life's small enjoyments by sharing them with their friends. This is a very simple way of releasing tension, and it explains why women are more likely than men are to become shopaholics, as mentioned previously. These are among the simple things in life that do not require scientific testing.

Energy is felt most powerfully on our wedding days or when we win big prizes. Energy surges through our bodies, and it is little wonder we say a bride "glows." What we usually forget is that we could use this same good feeling and fill our bodies up on it if only we would stop and do this for a few seconds at those other times when we feel that nice feeling surging through us.

When we win prizes or pass exams, get promoted, or go on a holiday, that's when these feelings will surge through us. Unfortunately, we generally forget to stop and allow that feeling to flow through our bodies therefore we rarely consciously feel it. When we do feel it for an instant, we immediately distract ourselves with a "What's next?" diversion.

Below are some examples of feel-good feelings that come from many activities. Try to implement some of these in your life with greater frequency, and you will see the difference it makes every day. You'll feel easier and freer about most things in life, including yourself. Energy flow is the operative word; it's the same energy flow in sex, as I have discussed above and in these examples below.

- **Work** : Stop when you feel a job is well done. Breathe this feeling in and allow yourself to acknowledge this.
- **Acupuncture for energy distribution**: This gives you a renewed energy feeling that actually aligns your energy. Get a treatment at least every eight weeks for good internal balancing.
- **Success**: Feelings of success makes you feel good because you are producing results you are happy about. Stop for a moment and allow yourself to feel this feeling, even with small successes.
- **Family**: When family situations make you feel good, try and stop to appraise your small wins in life and simply acknowledge a good deed you may have done or received from a loved one.
- **Lack of feel-good feelings**: This causes distress and tension, so remember to be more aware when these negatives pop up, make a decision to stay present, and correct this negative habit by simply letting it pass after, you have noted its presence, like you would a smelly fart. You don't want to keep smelling it after it's gone, do you? Choose to see negative feelings in the same way.

- **Creative hobbies**: Take stained glass, painting, baking, or woodworking class; join an antique collecting group, a car or hobby club.
- **Outdoor activities**. Regularly go for a walk, swim, dance, participate in a sport, or join a charity you can give some time to— all very fulfilling.
- **Yoga**: Taking up yoga results in good feelings and reduces heart, prostate, and many other issues; regular classes seem to balance the body easily and naturally.
- **Meditation**: Meditation provides the feeling of greater ease, relaxation, and general contentment all because your breathing slows. The even flow of energy allows the body to rebalance, creating regeneration on a cellular level.

Personal Hygiene Most Males Neglect: Foreskin Sensitivity

Many men develop irritation inside the foreskin and simply put up with it, figuring it's a normal part of how it feels after ejaculation. Incorrect. This is a very prominent issue, as there seems to be a large percentage of men who have this problem and don't know how to alleviate it.

Drops of urine, sperm fluid, and perspiration accumulate under the foreskin. A rinse under the shower is generally not enough, and this is how most men accumulate a strong odour inside their foreskin. Guys; just pull your foreskin down after going to the loo; a quick rinse is so easy and will avoid all build up that generally happens during the course of the day. And don't forget the 'surprise quickie' with that possible… encounter will put the partner off due to your lack of awareness of your habitual odour.

Foreskin Case 1 – A 20yr old client complained of extreme sensitivity at his foreskin after ejaculation and admitted he'd never tried to pull his foreskin down. I asked him if he wanted this situation to continue until he was in his forties or if he wanted to correct it? He didn't want his discomfort to continue and admitted it was embarrassing.

He later told me he discovered underneath the foreskin a white, cheesy crust, as though his penis had been soaking in a bath for two weeks.

Foreskin Case 2 - Another unbelievable case I've came across was a thirty-nine-year-old tradesman. He was complaining about the sensitivity he had with his foreskin but said he had never pulled it down only noticed redness that was painful. I could not imagine what condition his thirty-nine-year-old penis was in after thirty years without being cleaned under the foreskin, and I was not going to try to talk sense with this man and just suggested he see a doctor.

Essentials for Male Hygiene—Solutions for Sensitive Skin

If you have had redness inside the foreskin and are very sensitive to touch, this means you customarily don't wash there, and bacteria builds up, making it sensitive. A quick water rinse will generally do, but if you consistently neglect to wash thoroughly, you need a more thorough washing. Pull the foreskin down completely when you're in the shower and wash it with soap a few times. After you have dried yourself, rub a couple of drops of olive oil around the head, inside the foreskin. Cold-pressed olive oil retains many nutrients, thus making it a pleasant lubricant that in turn heals the irritation. Your penis will be protected from odour and irritation for a whole day, and you will always have a fresh, clean, and protected member. No scientific research is necessary here! This not only prevents odour but also eliminates sensitivity. As soon as you begin to wash regularly, all the redness and infection will gradually fade, and your penis will go back to being nice and rosy.

Extreme sensitivity or prolonged redness means the condition is advanced, as thorough washing has been avoided. In that case, apply the oil twice times daily after quick rinses. This will very quickly eliminate all bacteria and sensitivity, and you won't believe how you feel and how comfortable and enjoyable your sexual experiences will be from then on.

For serious problems with sensitivity or foreskin tightness, see a doctor! Certain creams can stretch the foreskin and make it much softer. However, the natural method above does the trick in the vast majority of cases.

Guys love "getting head" and think about this often, but how many guys think about the cleanliness of their genitals? Perspiration causes odour, but several visits to the toilet during the day will tip the scales. The best way to know how clean you really are is to look at your underwear, which will always tell the story of how clean you keep yourself in the privates department. Guys can also lightly shave their genital areas. This makes it so much more pleasing to their ladies, and really helps to keep the build up of odour to a minimum.

A famous Chinese female comedian related to a huge crowd how gay men are known for their genital cleanliness far more than are straight males. Interesting point!

To Conclude: People are rarely aware of the need to stop and allow themselves to feel the good feelings that can come from simple pleasurable experiences. They don't recognize them in simple things; instead, they strain to grasp this from outside. As a consequence, males especially carry tension and stress, which builds up as a result of not being able to integrate these everyday nice feelings they could easily connect to.

If only we would stop for a few seconds to feel that nice feeling surging through us, and train ourselves to take note when that feeling arises. This is what "stop and smell the flowers" means. It's a simple way of replacing stress quickly, easily, and pleasurably; we just have to make it a habit.

Why Men Cheat on Women

Cheating is so misunderstood. Most men go to adult services out of pure need and feel very guilty as a result. This is usually because their wives or partners are absorbed with work or busy with children.

When a wife has young children, she's normally so engrossed that she overlooks her husband's needs. Of course, some understanding is necessary on the husband's part, as his wife is giving all her energy to the little ones. Men generally understand this, but it does not take away his need to release built-up tension.

Every woman needs to ask herself, "How long do I want to keep my man, until my children are in their teens? Do I want to celebrate their twenty-first birthdays with the whole family"?

As children begin to develop interests and become teens, their parents' focus shifts to more-serious issues regarding their schooling and work capabilities. As a result, the husband-wife situation takes a back seat, and neither partner may be giving the attention to the other's needs.

Men need nurturing from their women, and a woman's nurturing is what keeps her man attached to home and family and prevents him from straying. Women may think it's their looks or sexiness, hair, perfume, or cooking that draws men. It's a combination of all those things, but the one factor that stands out for men is how much satisfaction they're getting in the bedroom. If they aren't 'getting' enough, they will very likely start looking elsewhere.

A man doesn't wander without cause, and it's not because he doesn't love his partner—it's because when his tension is not released, he is stressed by it, and he will either masturbate his tension away or want a woman to do it for him; this is all he can think about until his tension is released. If his partner is frequently unwilling, he may end up going to adult services.

Is the Effort of Giving Him a Quickie
Worth Losing Your Man Over?

If a man's partner is astute enough, she will recognize his need and agree to his request for a "quickie." In the long run, this will save her marriage. Women love to find fault with their men and chastise them for many things only because they don't understand or do things their way. But when they lose their man, all the blame comes out.

Women generally don't realize it's no big deal to give her man a quickie if this is all he really wants. He doesn't go shopping for a new hairstyle or face cream like women do to give themselves a quick pick-me- up. A man's happiness comes from feeling relieved, and there is no better way for him to feel relieved than with a quickie, if that is all he can get at that time. For women, it's more about fulfilment, and they can easily get this from a bit of shopping and sharing with girlfriends. Unless they are gay, men of every nationality don't discuss their shopping and purchases with other guys.

What relaxes men most, and what they love above all else, is the warm touch of his woman, her appreciation, and her nice gestures. There are many funny jokes about how easy it is to please a man; ladies, we are the ones who are hard to please. We want and demand and expect, and slowly the guys find this all too hard and just want some time away from the demands that work generally puts on them, without having to listen to any more from us. They get together for sports and drinks to feel free of their many tasks and obligations as providers.

The reason an older man will seek a young girl's companionship, is that she just does not have the analytical insights that have scrutinized him at home. He will find it simpler to have a more superficial interaction with a younger female, who is far less complicated. His search for distraction and the reason for his slowly turning away, to find and have his needs satisfied elsewhere begin here.

This is the truth, ladies, and it's far more likely this is what your men have considered if they haven't already gone to adult services without your knowing it. Consider how much easier it is for a man to go to adult services and get some satisfaction than it is to wait again and again and to be made to feel all he wants is sex?

Why Males Look for Release - Men will frequently begin to look elsewhere for releasing stress when they don't know why their mates have seemingly withdrawn from them. If they only knew how women are really turned on when their man is connected to his *heart* during love play and intimacy, this could prevent so much secrecy and frustration and enrich relationships instead. Life works when we are balanced, but it goes out of kilter when we're in disharmony with ourselves. How do we overcome this cycle? How can we gain balance?

The easiest way we can balance our lives is by taking charge of our lives so the build-up doesn't continue. The problem for most husbands is they generally experience real guilt and hope their wives will not find out they're going outside to release their built-up tension. In some cases, hope their partners will be understanding enough to give them more sexual pleasure.

What Can You Do to Help Your Man, Ladies? How often do you go up to your man and say lovely things to him, thank him for the little things he might have done for you, or better still, how often do you take turns giving one another oral? These are all very important matters to consider when you love your partner, or, more to the point, if you really wish to keep him.

If your partner is indeed precious to you and sex is not as important to one of you, you both need to choose alternative methods, like an occasional foot massage, neck massage, or hand relief. These are such simple means that don't have to turn into prolonged sexual interludes.

The one thing that will really turn your man on is acknowledgement of how much work he does. That way he will crave your loving rather than just sex, and he will beg you to give him more tenderness. Tenderness doesn't always need to lead to something sexual. To avoid sexual innuendo, you just need to say "I'm going to give you a neck, (foot, hand, or shoulder) massage for a few minutes before dinner or during the movie." These simple "punctuation marks" can help you maintain a successful relationship.

Massage is an activity you can share, you could plan to take turns once a month to keep it fresh and novel. The sexual release he needs could be arranged as a compromise quickie this simple act can go a long way to release some tension and provide the TLC (tender loving care) that men really need from their partners. This will focus your man on what you can share and satisfy his needs rather than his entertaining ideas of seeking satisfaction elsewhere.

To Conclude : The best attention you can give your man is nurturing from time to time. When men get involved with family and receive nurturing from their partners, they are not likely to seek sex outside the home. Receiving a little nurturing from your partner is an easy method to cultivate and create a healthy habit and a nurturing relationship.

Chapter 2

Your Internal Power Source

This power inside us, when activated, gives us feelings of joy and exhilaration, a buzz all over, a blissful feeling. We generally get it through pleasurable experiences be they personal relationships or entertainment. Men and women seek these pleasures in different ways. Winning money activates this pleasurable feeling inside us, as do holidays, sexual intimacy, and a variety of celebrations. We all love a variety of events and adventures because of the good feelings we derive from them. As I've said before as soon as the good experiences end, so do the good feelings so to compensate for the loss of these feelings, we try temporary diversions. Lets explore how to maintain these good feelings.

It's balance we all seek, and we attain it from one another's experiences through learning and observation. We are actually spiritual beings having a human experience, and deep down inside we are loving beings, constantly becoming more human. Our task is to realize this and awaken to it consciously. When we come to this awareness, we automatically seek balance in our lives and naturally want to serve one another, as this is part of our internal 'god being' makeup.

Getting to a balanced place in your life is something you can easily learn to switch on and eventually you will be able to compare it in the same way as you would turning on a switch. This might sound a bit simplistic, but it's easily achievable and allows you to stay on top of any situation with a few minutes of daily practice. For example, staying fresh for the day, you spend some time in the shower. It's the same thing if you wish to stay in charge of your health and vitality; you would put some time aside daily to recharge your energy, as you will see when I discuss this further.

The illusion is that while we disbelieve our ability, we run around seeking this harmony from things outside of ourselves and are constantly duped by our minds, believing we don't have this internal power. This lack of awareness is brought about by false values and overly stressed competition.

A fast-track method of attaining balance involves working with the Law of Attraction how to press the "magic" buttons to access your marvellous internal power.

Those who have found this balance tell us they no longer struggle as they did—their lives become easy, and money starts to flow. The 'Law of Attraction' was the subject of the 2008 documentary *The Secret*, portrayed in the four Oprah shows that took the world by storm.

The Higher Pleasure for Males

This higher aspect within us is actually our inner strength, and it is what we are all here to awaken to. As men are more connected to strength and supportive elements in their relationships, they need the higher emotional aspect they get from looking to their woman to acknowledge this gentle part within them.

When men seek connections with women, they desire not only to dominate them but also to be inspired by them. This ancient law is depicted in the Tarot card that symbolizes the Lovers. The woman is looking to the angel above the couple because deep down, a 'woman' is connected to the 'higher angelic' aspect or healing power within her. The man looks toward the woman, connecting with his higher aspect through the female, that way he is connecting to 'his feminine side' through her. The Authors; Rider and Waite, created the most referenced tarot deck known as: The Rider- Waite Tarot Deck, by U.S. Games Systems, Stamford Publishers. The 'Rider Waite Tarot' is the most widely recognized Tarot deck, and the first deck published in the 20th century. It was created by members of the Hermetic Order of the Golden Dawn, and is especially suited to questions of a mystical nature. This tarot deck has the original symbolism that all other tarot card artists have copied. Now there are well over a thousand copied versions of tarot cards by artists throughout the world, and most of them have used the Ryder and Waite deck from the late 1800's to glean their own version of symbolism. See: http://www.facade.com/tarot/rider_waite/

Owning Your Power

Many laws govern our lives. One of them is whatever you focus your mind upon you bring into your life. This internal law applies to both positive and negative aspects of our reality. Therefore, if you fear something will happen, you are unwittingly drawing it closer to you. This law applies to absolutely everything. For example, you're looking out for police car whilst speeding, and suddenly one appears. Another example: you're secretly admiring someone's partner or a nice figure and not realizing at the same time that deep down, regretful feelings may be at play. When you feel this way about anything in your life, you are really evoking a sense of lack within you, a sense of "I don't have." You are pushing away the very thing you want because you are focusing on *what you don't have,* the negative part, thereby stimulating the *I don't have* feeling, which attracts to you the very situation you don't want, because you are replaying this negative feeling. When you stay un-aware of doing this you will stay in that same un fulfilled feeling/situation and money and progress will evade you.

This is the same Law of Attraction, whatever you focus upon goes both ways, so if you focus on the negative you will draw that to you equally as strongly. It's the same as using electricity as an example, its not going 'to judge' how you use it, it works in whatever way you employ its power, to warm up your home or to destroy something.

A Movie Perspective of Relationships

How wonderful we feel when we meet someone new and experience that warm, excited feeling. As the relationship unfolds, we think *this is the one.* As we begin to imagine a wonderful future, the excitement builds and pleasurable feelings develop. So why does it so often not turn out the way we expected? We are all so different; wouldn't it be great to have signals of what to be aware of to avoid the pitfalls and traps that lead us astray in relationships?

Let's take a viewer's seat in a cinema as a movie plays. Imagine you are taken to the scenario of your life relationships, showing you step by step how they all unfolded from when you were a young child hearing and listening to everything your parents say every day—their opinions, frustrations, and anxieties. As this plays out before your innocent eyes, it all becomes imprinted on your psyche and your developing personality. You unwittingly become shaped by your parents' opinions and passions, positive and negative. As you grow up, not suspecting this moulding has taken place, you go into the world and meet people socially and professionally and have no idea why you react to certain situations the way you do.

Have you ever been in a situation in which you've been caught up in a relationship that became negative or addictive, where you or your partner felt out of control, causing your business life, or worse, your marriage to suffer?

Often we look to doctors, alcohol, holidays, shopping, money, or stories to somehow justify the situation at hand. We say "I'm just tired" or "I need a holiday" to alleviate our problems. Yet somehow, the holiday only temporarily relieves us because we have failed to address long-dormant issues, and we find ourselves in the same familiar situations. These temporary 'solutions' and our stories are methods of avoiding facing and making changes. Creating change means looking at what we've been denying. It may even mean giving up addictions, but mostly it means identifying and ending roles we play and have become stuck in usually to get attention the only way we know how.

How Do We Change the Movies of Our Pasts?

Go back to the beginning of the movie, when you were a child. Observe the way a parent behaved when you were not acknowledged or unappreciated. The child in you 'discovered a behaviour'. As un-resourceful as it was, it was a way of getting the attention you needed in a way that worked back then. But now it no longer works, because everything has changed—your age, the people around you and their circumstances—so how do we release these 'stuck' patterns that detract from our adult relationships, and most important, how do we tap back into our power, especially if relationships seems to have a hold on us?

One way is to start by identifying when a recurring negative situation has come up again. Just by identifying it rather than reacting to it, you begin to create positive change, which starts with awareness. For example; when you are with a person who generally presses your buttons, try listening to what he or she is saying and respond thoughtfully rather than racing to justify by reacting. This big key will allow you to recognize you do have control and are the only person who can stop the knee-jerk repetition.

Retaining this awareness is how you will fall out of this insidious habit or "monkey mind." Constant awareness and vigilance on your part will help you say no to this un-resourceful, habitual way of interacting.

This is the key to your success and to overcoming negative habits. You can beat anything with persistent application.

Choice is always in your hands. Ask yourself if you want to stay in this state or step out and feel more energized and joyful. By making a disciplined and intended effort to change, you will change your relationship with yourself, and you will find your relationships with others will begin to operate on these newly discovered foundations. Rather than staying in reactive tendencies steeped in childhood conditioning, your interactions with people will become warmer, and you will have more friendly connections, the same as your connection with yourself. Taking responsibility for your happiness is the key to owning your power in relationships; this fact becomes obvious as you maintain a positive attitude. Lack of awareness prevents us from recognising that feel good feelings come from inner satisfaction and from simple validation.

Your Internal Computer

Human consciousness is like an internal computer. It responds not only to goals we set for ourselves, but it can also achieve miracle cures and impossible feats. All we need to do is decide we really want to go the distance and set a target.

In the movie *127 Days*, an unfortunate situation turned into a miraculous one. A mountaineer who had fallen into a crevasse had to cut his arm off with a blunt knife or die, as his arm was pinned under a rock for six days. Like a computer that is programmed, so has our internal consciousness been programmed since we were children. The same way as we can delete computer programs, applies also the internal programs in our consciousness. The young man who cut off his arm had to listen to the only positive voice (program) he had inside him to survive. He was first led to the edge of his own existence and needed to give up all his mental objections in order to undertake the horrifying ordeal to save himself.

Most of us give in to our negative voices. We do not proceed with the obvious that is staring us in the face but instead take the easy way out, even though it will prolong our agony. We all need to come to the very edge of our tolerance before we can let go of the shackles and step into the part of life we have been reaching for.

Not all of us know how to operate complicated computer programs; most of us need a computer expert to do this for us. It's no different with human consciousness. Not all of us know how to operate the system inside us, which is a hundred thousand times more complicated than a computer. Hence, this book will help you navigate to the results you want! Not all of us will need to know how to use the common Photoshop program; likewise, in our consciousness we have an internal program version of 'inner tuition' directed from our higher selves our intuition, directing us all the time. It is through learning to listen to it that we will get the best guidance. Stilling ourselves for an hour in meditation once a week will help us get in touch with this inner guidance and can easily be achieved with a relaxing yoga class.

Aaron, the young man who had fallen into the crevasse, finally gave up his struggle after his horrendous six-day ordeal. Only then did he have an amazing internal vision that opened up his inner eye. He saw himself in a future situation as a father with a little boy running into his arms. At that moment, he also saw he was without his forearm. This was what spurred him on to do the unthinkable.

Pure Joy Is the Beginning

Pure joy is what we are all about. We all seek joy in various activities, for example, satisfaction with something we are doing, creating, or sharing, or being recognized for accomplishing something special. If it wasn't for the joy factor driving us, we wouldn't be able to complete projects, build homes, watch games, or play sports. Joy gives us the enthusiasm to go on with our activities. Without the element of fun, we wouldn't start anything. Sometimes we put our lives at risk with extreme sports or drugs to get a feeling of ecstasy when we cannot get this from our lives. We all strive for joy in some way—it seems to be a common factor for us all—so let's get a better understanding what this feeling is that we all crave so much and learn how to access it at will!

Pure joy is pure energy. We see it in children and in the Olympic games, when joy reaches excellence in expression. Think about the expression on someone's face when he or she wins a million dollars or watches a romantic movie; such movies stimulate that sassy, invigorated sensation or we wouldn't watch them. We enjoy excellence just as we enjoy feeling joyful. We have this pure energy of joy inside us, so why don't we always feel it? Where does this feeling go, and how do we get it back? Why do we become ill, and why do all those negative emotions arise? Wouldn't it be great to have this joy on call, being able to turn up our energy at will? Let's take a moment to identify where this energy source comes from to begin with.

To Conclude: Simply stilling yourself for an hour or in meditation helps you get in touch with your inner guidance to challenging life's problems. This can be easily achieved and avoids much frustration and searching. It increases awareness and promotes feel-good feelings that come from inner satisfaction and leads to balance and joyfulness.

Discovering Sexual Energy as Your Power Source

When switching your car on, you know it's the motor that gets it going, and you would never think of putting a mixture of water and oil into the petrol tank, would you? The 'petrol tank' within us is our minds, yet we fuel our minds with all kinds of rubbish. No wonder we don't feel well. The source of our personal energy is at the base of the spine, which is associated with our sexual energy. Because we have labelled it and isolated it as sexual energy only, we don't really know it could be our *main power switch.*

The secret is that unlike sexual activity, this power can last. Usually when that energy is activated, it feels good for the duration of the sexual experience, then (in males) dissipates soon after, leaving them wanting this experience all over again. It is little wonder pornography has become a multibillion-dollar industry; it associates sex with the sexual act only, instead of recognizing its potential that can cause feelings of vibrancy and energy and balance in health and vitality, which is the real secret behind sex !

Persistent Sexual Arousal Syndrome—PSAS

This unfortunate condition has certain women's bodies on constant sexual alertness. These women crave and need sexual satisfaction constantly and are very embarrassed by their demands. No man can keep up with his ongoing daily demands, and he will eventually feel worn out by them.

The unfortunate part is, that when some women have found partners who love sex as much as they do and can satisfy them, they still don't solve their problem, which is ongoing. While it may fascinate men to have women in constant arousal, and some men may be able to perform to those needs, three major aspects remain overlooked.

First, the more frequently a man ejaculates, the faster he will age, as he is constantly unloading his sperm fluid, which is tied up with internal emotion. In the long term, this will drain him whether or not he feels it in the short term. Males generally agree that ejaculating causes them to feel drained afterward. Sperm is life force, and draining it away frequently, is an energy loss that does not benefit the body. This is a common comment that many of my clients have expressed to me in a variety of ways. So I have summed up some of their comments here:-

- If I don't ejaculate, I have more drive…
- They don't have to tell me in Tantra classes that ejaculation, drains your life force or energy, I can feel it.
- Some Tantra classes teach you how to have an orgasm without ejaculation using breathing techniques, its nice when I can do it.
- Every time I ejaculate, I feel a little less drive for a few days, but when I don't ejaculate for a few days, I feel more motivated.

Unfortunately, some males get frustrated with the breathing techniques and don't realize how they can help. The common comment is that Tantra does not teach them how to last longer in the bedroom, which is what every male is after!

Second, knowledge of the chakras solves this situation. For women with PSAS, their base and sacral centre chakra or energy centre is overly alerted and using a lot of their energy; hence, their energy is unbalanced. By simply balancing their energy, it will gradually, with deliberation and perseverance, rebalance. The method is very simple: meditation and focusing on internal energy and seeing it gradually move up the body.

This is all explained with the technique in www.theorgasmiceffect.com

Just because the energy is stuck does not mean it has to stay that way! With deliberation and focus, we can slowly make it flow naturally. The body obeys all our commands—we just haven't been taught this. We ARE in charge of our bodies, which is the main message in these pages!

Third, such a constant need as in PSAS whether satisfied or not it is an addiction. Do you really want this or any addiction to rule your life? An addiction will eventually pass and will not last into your sixties, you will have a lot more life to live after that.

Coming down off any addiction leaves people with an empty feeling, as they have identified with that addiction for some time. After it's gone, they are left not knowing who they are or what to do as they have limited their lives to the narrow window of sensory gratification only. The chakra links in the next few paragraphs explain the natural flow of how our energy moves via the chakra system.

Development of Our Sexual Energy

Before puberty, energy circulates throughout the body, without direction. At puberty, it's awakened and slowly becomes polarized into sexual energy. We sporadically use it in sex, but it stays mostly in the sexual region. A better way to understand what we call sexual energy is to look at the energy centres in our bodies. Each centre has a specific function, and when all centres are aligned with positive energy, we can say we have a sense of vibrancy, which translates as joy and vitality. Vibrancy is something we can actually feel, and it can be observed in athletes.

You can get a quick overview here by looking at the chakra system, which is a map of your energy centres: http://www.chakraenergy.com/. You can raise your energy through the chakras in the same way you can rev the engine in your car. In a similar way, you can raise the energy within the chakras by simply focusing on each one specifically. (I'll discuss a little later where the chakras are located and how to get a positive buzz within the chakras.)

You can find a comprehensive, easy reference to the chakra system at: http://www.healer.ch/Chakras- e.html. This is nicely explained and easy to follow and will give you understanding of how important our energy centres are and will teach you how to keep them healthy to maintain balance.

Most-frequently asked questions are, "How do I think of something positive when I'm in a bad mood or having a bad day?" and "Why not just use sex to feel good in the conventional way of having sex?" You could, but if life was about feeling good all the time and all you had to do was have sex or eat, you could solve everything that way.

Most of us have discovered we need to have some sort of emotional connection to our partners to be completely satisfied by sex. People seek long-term relationships to have ongoing connections that develop into deeper sharing, with sex being part of the total package.

Sexual activity is built-up sexual tension tied up with emotion. When this emotional tension has built to a maximum, it is converted into fluid in males and ejaculated. All emotions—joy, laughter, exhilaration, and grief—ultimately get converted into fluid.

When men release sexual energy, they feel tired and pleasantly euphoric, but this doesn't last very long. The satisfying euphoric sensation for females can last up to an hour. Let's discover why this difference exists between males and females.

The Benefit of Sexual Energy

When sexual energy spreads throughout the body, all the cells and organs in the body are energized, and the whole body benefits. This happens naturally in children. Children involved in play involve all their energy. They don't sit back and say, "I'm tired now. I want to have a rest," as adults do after sexual activity.

In this same way, by raising your sexual energy and spreading it through your body, you can energize all your organs instead of just the sexual centre. This benefits and energizes your body's energy system, which is what happens with women. When a woman orgasms, the feeling floods her body and she feels energized, alive, and relaxed as a result of the full-body orgasms many women experience.

When men orgasm, rather than that feeling spreading through their bodies, as it does with women, the feeling lasts only a few minutes. This is the result of a genital climax, so they can never get the great feeling to last as women do. Watching how women stay in the prolonged orgasmic state is what increases males' fascination for pornography that depicts how women can stay in that state for a prolonged time. Learning the techniques I've mentioned gives men the full-body orgasm, increased satisfaction and overall greater vitality in addition to the ability to last as long as they want to every time. When practiced daily, it changes the body energy dynamic and vitality levels forever. Some males have described the change as a whole new mind set. See www. theorgasmiceffect.com.

How Athletes Depend on Their Energy Stimulus

Athletes say they get the same endorphin release levels from exercise as women get from their full-body orgasm experiences. When they push themselves to the limit they get stimulated by the "gain from the pain" endorphin rush that follows.

The Australian Olympic champion swimmer Ian Thorpe talked about the endorphin release he would get when finally all the pain would stop and the pleasurable feeling flooded his body until this was what he aimed for every time. Extreme sports participants aim for this same rush.

When we regularly exercise, we generally experience a nice feeling because of the endorphins released in our bodies. Imagine getting this release without all the exercise. Doing this involves discovering the magic buttons, a bit like watching someone driving a car and saying, "That's easy. It's only pushing two pedals and turning the wheel." But everyone knows that while driving looks simple, it takes time and practice and is more than just pushing pedals and turning the wheel to do so safely and properly. Like anything worthwhile, you really want to put all your effort into attaining that skill and getting that sense of accomplishment and the good feelings that come with it.

To Conclude: By balancing your energy, your feelings of emptiness give way to joy energy whether from sexual intimacy or sports activity. The more connected you are with yourself, the more balanced your emotions are, and you will feel more energized, rather than feeling something is missing at the end of it all, as people feel when satisfying an addiction.

Your Mind and Your Being

Making the distinction between your mind and your being is the key and the secret, to owning your power. It's that 'inner state' without which life is a mere shadow. The ability to work with our emotional state is always at our fingertips and ever present. It's the key to energy control and self-empowerment. This remains an elusive secret until the individual unlocks this 'secret power within' and recognizes that fact. See 'The Chakra System' Pg. 69

Our minds are our tools, and part of the mind's function is to make decisions and choices. We generally remember events by making pictures of our experiences through vision. The more significant the experience, the more senses are involved and the more indelibly the memory of the experience is imprinted on our minds.

Take a good joke for example. The better the joke, the more vivid the picture the person is portraying, and we usually laugh because of what we are 'picturing'. This is the mind working with memory, and the more experiences we have, the more pictures we have in our memories. Our minds access these internal pictures as 'frames of reference' when we visualize anything. That's how a joke becomes funny. We laugh at our frames of reference presented by our minds; this is why a younger mind may not get a joke, having not as many frames of life's experiences and references.

Examples of Our Memory References

A thief has different frames of reference than a doctor has. A farmer has different frames of reference than a dressmaker, and so on. The mind builds up references or pictures that help or hinder us according to how frequently we have imprinted the images connected with our experiences as pictures, or 'frames of references', upon our minds since childhood.

Childhood pictures stay with us and help or hinder us according to how pleasurable or destructive they were. If the memory has been suppressed—usually due to an unpleasant experience that never surfaced—it will usually play havoc with our lives down the road. When negative experiences have not been addressed and released through some form of therapy or courses, those unpleasant experiences generally produce negative responses with any type of relationship, business or personal. This is depicted in *Marnie,* a movie with a young Sean Connery and Tippi Hedren that takes you through the story of his uncovering his wife's tragic childhood and the riveting twists when it's finally brought to the surface.

Difference between Your Being and Your Mind "State"

Your being is your natural state. For example, you'd never say, "I'm doing a friend" or "I'm doing a holiday" or "I'm doing in love." You would say, "I'm being in love," or "I'm being on a holiday," or "I'm being with a friend!" When you are just being yourself, not pretending or being superficial, you are being real or honest without the thinking process. When a person is being real, a certain resonance comes across. When a person is not being real, there is uncertainty, restraint, and avoidance. Generally, the person is not fully present, possibly because he or she is withholding something. Everyone can notice lack of openness, a holding back perceived as avoidance.

An example is when you're not connecting with your partner—perhaps sex is not very exciting, or you are withholding something and avoiding communication. This is when you are not fully engaged with your energy, it's when you are not in your 'being' state but rather, in your mind. The mind is discerning, it processes, judges, criticises and analyses, the being state is open and full of wonder and creativity...It's that simple!

'Baggage' We Carry—Our Internal Frames of Reference

Children too have frames of reference, developed and stored according to their experiences and ages. Within their frames of reference are the values of their parents, which have become imprinted upon their minds through daily repetition. Negative memories of unfortunate experiences are more indelibly imprinted on their minds and become major frames of reference—for example, a physical punishment they may have endured, or a friend being killed in accident they may have witnessed.

We can compare frames of reference to movies in that they are collections of images from which we take our main references for life and store in 'memory banks'. These are references connected to our emotions and our visual and mental associations; they become our internal programs. We generally refer to negative states as the "baggage" we carry. We could also refer to them as "viruses," similar to computer viruses. Replaying negative emotions is connecting to negative images, which is staying stuck in life, a bit like dragging heavy baggage around. This can affect how we relate with others and ourselves and is a disempowering way of being in our life.

You could refer to these as viruses that need to be deleted, in order to connect to your wellness so you can have more joy and happiness that energizes you; which is your 'being' energy. The viruses in this example can prevent you from fully engaging with happiness and vitality. Another way of putting it for extra clarity is; animals have references and "memory banks" also, that are more associated with smell.

The negative references interfere with how open and fully honest we can be with ourselves; that opens access to our natural joy or "being" state. Our being states are our feelings or joyous states we refer to as our heart energy. Here is a good example of this: when saying "OMG!" or "Oh my God!" women will naturally place their hand on their heart as they seem to be more connected with their hearts and emotions, as this simple observation demonstrates. However when do we see men doing the same thing? This is a curious fact and even more curious is that it's males rather than females who have the frequently occurring heart problems that frequently lead to surgery.

Switching Off Your Negative Energy and Owning Your Power

Balancing your mind and your being is not quantum physics; in fact, it's very easy. It's all part of unveiling the secret of the power within and wanting to be in charge rather than have someone else pushing your negative buttons.

When you're 'swimming in the river in Egypt' (de Nile or denial), always ask yourself, "How long do I want to stay in this un-resourceful state? Would I like to step out of this 'river of bad feelings' to feel the real me, which is my unlimited energized being state, or inner being, or am I still addicted to these feelings and not ready to take that step of addressing what is holding me back?"

If this un-resourceful feeling builds up, it can slowly turn into regret, jealousy, melancholy, or other disempowering feelings. When people are not very aware of themselves, they may not realize they're stuck in a situation of their own making, seeing the world through coloured glasses. They may have come to feel safe in their thoughts that this is the way life is.

By comparing ourselves with someone else in a similar situation and replay their dialogues of what happened to them, is avoiding facing our own emotions and what we may need to do. You would then end up falling short of your own desires, if you keep repeating the familiar dialogues in your mind that you are so used to identifying with, worth pondering over.

When people are not aware of their internal dialogues, they can stay in disempowered states for many years. When they become more aware, they begin to recognize that the dialogue has become something of a habit they've grown accustomed to and have allowed to go unchecked, becoming like a never-ending CD they haven't switched off in their head.

Taking control: You can begin to take control and own your inner power and step into your 'being state'! Here is a quick and easy way of doing so:

As soon as you notice a message repeating in your head that is not a positive one, ask yourself what specifically do you want to change in your life and what specific gains would you like to have with this change?

When aliveness is missing in a person's life, he or she may feel a sense of emptiness or even a deadening feeling. Indulging in drugs or drinking is a common way of avoiding dealing with this unaddressed, built- up pain. Here is a nice quote from Bob Proctor and Mary Morissey's CD series "Working with the Law".

> I toy in the domain of confusion when
> I don't let myself know what I really know,
> so I don't have to do what I want to do, when I
> don't let myself know what I really do know

To Conclude: Our minds picture things and record images, while our feelings tell us how we may feel about something. When we suppress past hurtful feelings, our minds record the event as a frame of reference. Replaying hurtful situations keeps negative frames of reference alive. This can easily be remedied with awareness and choosing to make changes to an ongoing habit.

How Your Mind Completely Controls Your Life

Keep in mind how our internal programs run us: whatever we focus our minds on for any length of time, we are sure to manifest it in our lives. Sometimes feelings of lack are unconscious feelings, and deep down, when we feel we are lacking love, strength, warmth, integrity, harmony, and caring, we unconsciously manifest that into our present. This is all part of negative programs mentioned earlier we get used to. Over time, this habit becomes our behaviour and default program.

> The mind is but a master power that moulds and makes.
> Man is mind and evermore he takes the tool of thought
> and shaping what he will brings forth a thousand joys

or a thousand ills. He thinks in secret and it comes to pass our environment is but out looking glass. From - Bob Proctor's in his personal development series – 'The Winner's Image'.

An epiphany: Is when we finally separate our minds from our inner beings and awaken to the fact that we are not our minds, this is an epiphany. We can then realize we and only we have been in charge of our lives. We are the directors, producers, and actors on our own stages of changing events that we believed were real until the moment we awake from this dream. This can be an amazing revelation!

Balancing the Body—Harmonizing the Mind

At this stage, you may realize that only you can give a nice feeling to yourself. Only you choose how you feel it and how you relate to it. This opens a way for you to begin to harmonize your body on the inside— for example, by having a relaxing massage or some other nice treatment or simply taking some time off.

The opposite of harmonizing is being stuck. Stuck-ness is frozen emotion, being out of touch with life or being asleep on the inside. When people feel out of touch with themselves, they may need to 'feel' more in order to bring that feeling of aliveness back. Extreme sports and climbing in high-risk areas can be substitutes for creating aliveness, especially when individuals are out of touch with their souls or inner-being states.

We seem to have lost the ability to stimulate our bodies with the aliveness of gentleness and love and true feelings of caring and sharing, and so we turn to exaggerated materials such as you find in movies. This is when having a massage, feeling good through touch, is so important for your body. What a massage really does is activate or stimulate your energy from within, while you are relaxing.

Getting Fulfilment from Your "Power Source" or Sexual Energy

Children run around full of vibrant energy pulsating through them because their energy is not localized as it is in adults, so they have not begun to interpret and analyse their energy with their minds. They don't stop and think; they just go with the energy pulsating through their bodies. We adults usually experience this pulsating energy as sex because it has become localized in our head and genital areas.

We can rename this energy by recognizing that it's the very same vibrant sexual energy within us. When we have sex, do we analyse what we are doing in the middle of it? Hopefully not. This vibrant energy starts expanding from the base of the spine and can spread up through the rest of the body.

In yoga, or Tantra, this energy is aroused where people begin to feel this energy moving up their bodies. 'I coined' the phrase; 'The Orgasmic Effect' because this is exactly what happens. Dancers and athletes experience this feeling frequently. When orgasmic energy is activated this way, an individual can feel that orgasmic feeling without having to go through the sexual process, so this can also occur even during meditation.

When you harness this energy, you become in charge of your energy and vitality and in control of your health and wellness of your body system. This is mentioned also in Buddhist practices and temples. I discuss this energy more fully in a later chapter, where I_address the Kundalini energy or serpent power, which is usually dormant at the base of the spine the chakra system.

Children have this energy on tap. When we as adults can finally release blockages that stand in the way of this powerful energy, we can then plug into and have this energy on tap just as easily and frequently as children do.

Abundant Joy Radiates from Your Core—
Your Pure Orgasmic Energy

In fact, 'radiating your energy' is very simple but it is not always easy to do for adults, because of the developed reasoning factor that interferes with the 'joy energy' of the inner child. Its easy to observe children radiating their energy, for us adults this powerful energy is connected with feelings of gratitude and appreciation, so when someone expresses appreciation to you, you open to that 'higher energy' or joy frequency. This usually happens unconsciously because it's the higher frequency that leaves you feeling elated.

Here is an example of this feeling of gratitude or elation. Imagine standing at the top of the Iguaçu falls in South America, the most majestic falls on our planet, or looking over the Grand Canyon in Arizona. You will definitely feel elation and expansion, feelings that come from deep within you, or your 'internal being' state. This is the being state children are switched into all the time and what we adults lose sight of because we do not take the time to activate the feeling of aliveness on any regular basis…. sadly to say.

The energy of joy stimulates the body; promotes vitality, longevity, and enthusiasm; and gives us emotional healing. This IS the pure 'Orgasmic Energy' that we can with practice 'switch on' at the core of our being!!

Identifying Love Energy

We all seek companionship. It doesn't matter who we are or where we are headed; companionship is part of our love and sharing energy. When we are not seeking it, we don't know how to share our love, or we may become very needy and want someone to provide it for us rather than share it. Relationships are based mainly on how we want others to give us the sharing and caring because we don't know how to give it or provide it for ourselves.

Love and sharing are placed in us from childhood, given in our 'mother's milk'. *It is what's not given and the degree to which it is withheld that determines how we have learnt to relate and perceive love.* This becomes indelibly imprinted and shapes our characters; it also determines how open or closed we are and how we see and relate in our relationships.

This same principle applies in animal behaviour; when baby animals have lost their mothers, they become withdrawn. Much rescue work today aims at rehabilitating baby animals and stray animals that suffer at the hands of uncaring people, especially poachers.

In a loving relationship, you have a connection with your heart that stimulates love, growth, and nurture; it's from here that health is maintained. Love is a cohesive force that connects our energy and acts as a rejuvenator for our whole system. Its interesting to note that this is what takes place naturally when a woman orgasms. She is recharged by an energy that is connected with love, and the part of her body that delivers this recharged feeling is the coccyx area, the seat of the Kundalini, where the serpent power resides. The chakras are all linked, the link below, will familiarize you with chakras and the Kundalini energy, where all the chakras are named with full descriptions: http://www.sacredcenters.com/chakras.

Playful energy is light-hearted energy, and it is important for adults to play during lovemaking and at other times, taking up an interest to connect with one's inner child. This is a major key to the light-hearted part of yourself, and connecting with child energy stimulates relaxation and ease. Sport and exercise, especially yoga, can do this; people generally feel good after yoga or some other light exercise class, and they especially feel good after sexual love play.

Years ago, when my girls were in their early teens, I'd walk on my hands on the beach. They'd run up, push me down, and say, "Mum, people are watching." I had to decide to wait until no one was watching or just do it. This decision allowed me to connect to my vibrant energy and give myself permission to engage in it more rather than less, as I grew older. My girls are now adults with lives of their own, and I still walk on my hands and do one-arm handstands with more people watching than before. I continue to feel fantastic because I ignored that very first constraint of what people would think.

When I dance or scuba dive, I rejoice, fully connecting to my child energy. I love the fun feeling, to rejoice, laugh and be silly like a child when I choose to.

We can all be silly and clown around and there are legitimate times to do so. We can, if we let ourselves, fun around like children by appropriating time for it. It's important to give ourselves permission to do so whether at a gym or during swimming, running, or any other sport. We should allow ourselves to let go without thinking someone is watching.

When We Are First Courting

You may recall how marvellous it was for the first six to twelve months of a relationship, when the sex was great. This is because of the chakras, which stimulate all the energy in the body were fully engaged, rather than just the genital area. The reason sex is so much more exciting in the beginning, is because of the level of anticipation appreciation and communication, especially eye contact that goes on without us really being aware of it. This simple connection naturally ignites all the body centres and is experienced at the heart chakra area. This is the big key we all miss not realizing it later on in life.

In the beginning, we are not consciously aware of this level of communication and gradually stop using it. When the search for a partner starts again, we don't realize how we never continued developing this further beyond the initial courtship stage. We didn't bring conscious awareness to continue using eye contact with our previous partner to keep that relationship alive, so we lose a simple ability that comes so easily in the beginning.

The key to keeping this connection alive between you and your partner is to remember what you may value or treasure about your partner as the relationship develops. When you look at your partner, do you generally express or acknowledge your appreciation or let him or her know how you feel about what they contribute and what you value about him or her? Adding a little personal touch in small things you do is so easy. Perhaps it is simply noticing and making a positive comment about how your partner may have gone out of the way for you with something they did recently. It's the fastest way to change the mood of any situation.

Sharing these feelings openly enables you to feel more deeply connected with yourself as well as your partner. It also gives you better, stronger health physically and emotionally and brings greater relaxation and spontaneity to your daily life.

When we act wholeheartedly, we bring our life energy into greater focus, enabling us to be more present to everything in our lives. Notice while playing with fun, childlike energy that you feel this energy physically. It's actually connected at the heart centre—your heart chakra.

To conclude: When you realize you and only you are in charge of your life, the actor on your own stage, you can change your reality by simply changing what you believed was real, simply by connecting with your heart. When you bring your heart into anything you do your way of interacting and seeing the world will change in an instant.

Using Sexual or Orgasmic Energy in Daily Life

When we enjoy something, we generally feel an energy that pulsates throughout our bodies. This is the reason we watch romantic movies or erotic sex; they give us the energized feeling everyone wants. We generally understand sexual energy as emotional tension usually followed by a pleasant euphoric sensation when released.

When we watch children get involved in activities, we notice how they use all their energy. Adult sexual energy is this same energy, except we have labelled it differently, thereby limiting our power or sexual energy. When we mature, this energy becomes_polarized, no longer circulating throughout the body. The energy now splits, and is focused in the head with the discerning logical mind and also at the lower sexual part of the body, therefore with adults we no longer experience it through the whole body as the child does. This marks the beginning of the aging process because as our energy is now divided we now separate ourselves from this natural joy, our pure energy.

Experiencing this wonderful energy in all its power throughout the body is actually what full-body orgasm is. By consciously raising your sexual energy, you can energize your body, gain greater control over your orgasms, and prolong your own and your partner's enjoyment. This has a positive effect on all levels because *'raising sexual energy is really getting involved in emotionally uplifting experiences more regularly'*.

When you engage in joyful activities, helping others without a motive, it helps the energy to spread throughout your body because you are acting from the heart and are focused on the heart. This raises your energy without you consciously being aware of it, thus energizing the body in this simple way! What an interesting study this would make…

Aliveness is our power and energy to either let go and feel free, or suppress this vitality, and only we have the power to do this, suppress or let go. This is the reason we need to release all negative patterns and programs first, as I mentioned earlier, so we may fully participate with our energy, which really is our inherent creative power.

There are so many benefits to plugging into our own power such as energizing our organs, increasing vitality, and improving self-esteem. This is why I keep pointing out that rather than localizing this energy in the sexual area as sexual experience, we can use this energy to stimulate our inner enthusiasm and joy for life whenever we like. Will expand on this is further in a later chapter. We can do so by connecting with quiet stillness and realize how amazing our bodies really are, that we are alive and can move and have free will, so many things people generally take for granted.

For example, when do we consciously stop and appreciate that we have people in our lives who love us and whom we love? Where would we be without people in our lives who love us? We forget to be grateful, and we forget to appreciate what we really have in life. When we regularly engage in appreciation, we quite literally raise our emotional energy levels instead of waiting for sex or for someone to appreciate us. Raising our energy levels in this way is the fastest and most direct way of maintaining our physical and emotional health, vital to our well-being.

An Exercise that Connects You to Orgasmic Energy

As I've previously mentioned because we don't often get to feel the 'higher notes' of appreciation and love, we often go for sex or drugs as the short cut to get the feel good feelings... Sexual energy is an emotion we can activate I have therefore listed below some exercises that give you a way of energizing your body and getting in touch with those great feelings you feel only in a relationship. It's like getting to play several musical notes on the scale; it will actually plug you into a lightness of joy, which increases steadily the more you practice the exercise.

Try this simple exercise: if for no other reason than to see how it works for you. Prolonging orgasm requires lifting your energy upward, raising your energy to the heart level. To do this without a sexual experience, try to put enjoyment into whatever you are doing; do it *with all your heart*, this will require focus with no distraction. You will need to silence your phone and decide what it is you want to do with all of your heart. It can be something quite mundane, such as humming as you walk. To give you an idea remember how you walk through a forest or beach or even being at a concert. The difference is when you're there, you are more fully engaged yes that's it; to be fully engaged, just try it now.

This simple routine will begin to change your energy and shift it from the mundane to a fresh joyful feeling that spreads through your body and slowly uplifts you, that is how it spreads throughout all your cells and why you feel elated. But you first need to give it a go and start in some small way, you can hum anywhere, it's a simple way to begin.

Orgasm is like that—it moves through the body, that's how the energy gets absorbed by all your cells. Any exercise you do can gradually connect you and put you in touch with the joy within. It sounds simple, and it is, *but most people haven't a clue they can maintain this connection outside sexual intercourse.* People can experience it as a joyful, exhilarating experience with any sport when their energy is high. Dancers regularly experience this. I felt I was having an orgasm quite literally when I came out of the water after my very first introductory scuba dive lesson.

Unfortunately, most males use sex for release from stress as a normal practice and have no idea it can be used for anything else. The above exercise can give males a calming effect and considerably reduce their tiredness and stress, so when they actually are ready for lovemaking, their mood will be greatly enhanced, and it will be lovemaking rather than just stress release, which often puts women off sex.

Express to your partner what you value or treasure most about her. Sincerely communicate through the eyes and express your feelings when you can even if it's just a simple acknowledgement about a nice meal preparation, just a comment here and there will increase the sexual mood between you. Notice how the other receives your genuine expression, and watch the shift in your sexual dynamic. You will see how easily it brings soothing feelings out and fond memories of your early days.

This is how you play the higher notes. This is the reason that sex was so much more exciting in the earlier days—your being was ignited and thankful for having met someone who could make you feel that special way. When you are not conscious of these higher notes or priceless gifts such as gratitude, caring, attention, and understanding and how these small things activate your tenderness, you simply forget and lose touch with why it worked before.

When you're totally present to all your emotions and not repressing them, positive or negative, this brings your life energy into greater focus, to everything. This is called owing your energy and enables you to be more receptive to your ultimate pleasures and joys of life. When we can accept all our emotions, we can stop judging ourselves and can give ourselves permission to accept love from others and love others more.

This openness intensifies our sexual experiences at a far deeper level than ever before.

The Difference between Women and Men When It Comes to Stress

Men generally agree they are disconnected, as though their genitals were separate from the rest of them. Why? Guys operate in their lives using logic. They talk about guy stuff, the game, their cars, their families and their work. Generally speaking, a family man is a provider and carries responsibility in his family or work. Men are traditionally breadwinners, and though nowadays women also take this role, when women take time off work to raise families, men usually take over as providers.

Guys are generally disconnected from their feelings because they operate from their rational, logical sides and focus on this part at work and home. They work hard and look forward to getting relief from built-up stress. They have mentally connected their need to release stress thru their genitals; this is how they release stress rather than discussing it with male friends. When men communicate amongst themselves they generally don't comment on how wonderful they look in their new shirts or shoes or how new hair products make their hair look.

This is where women are different. The first thing they do when they meet each other is compliment each other on how good they look or how nice their clothes or hair are. They go through these niceties even when they are not completely true; this is just the customary way women greet each other and get each other to feel good.

Hence, when women go out with each other for shopping or just catching up, they always like to exchange ideas on advice or share their little purchases. They generally love to share advice, compliments, and suggestions for styles, so when they get into relationships, they want all this from their men, but men find this difficult and don't know what they mean. They sometimes think their women are being hard to please when they insist on the trivialities they generally share with their women friends.

Women benefit from other women when it comes to addressing their social needs by releasing their stress; they don't have stress built up the way males do; they relate it through feelings. Males suppress their feelings until the tension builds up to the point that the only thing on their minds is genital relief.

Mothers obtain satisfaction by being needed by their children until they return to focusing on their own needs for personal satisfaction. This same nurturing need is what women express to one another in their socializing even though they are just sharing generally amongst themselves.

Males like to get involved with family needs to continue feeling needed, or they become more focused on their careers. They may feel ostracized by their partners when their partner is too busy with children and unknowingly disconnecting from their needs. This starts another cycle where men slowly begin to disconnect from their woman without really knowing it.

Ways of Keeping Your Energy Fresh

An exercise, that's not 'armchair' exercise, is a wonderful secondary support mechanism. A very simple way of creating mind-body balance is to begin an exercise routine such as yoga. This creates harmony in emotions and in health. Most forms of exercise—lifting weights, aerobics, Pilates, tai chi, dancing—are great; whatever you fancy, do it on a regular basis. I love scuba diving, but it's not something I can do frequently, so I choose things I can do regularly. You can choose ice hockey, ice skating, salsa or ballroom dancing, jazz, hip-hop, and the newest on the market, hula hooping; these are all good activities. Bush walking is a great way to socialize. The options are endless!

Whenever you have a particularly uplifting experience, stop and breathe the nice feeling in. It takes just two or three minutes, and your body will feel more revitalized with positive energy. Absorbing and breathing in this feeling nurtures and relaxes your body as you are doing it and you would be touching the orgasmic state. If it's not appropriate at the time, do it in the next hour or at the end of the day.

How Lack of Connection Affects You Sexually

Although men are generally turned on by sex at adult services, when asked if they enjoyed it, they will respond, "It was an empty feeling that lasted for only a few minutes and left me feeling cold" or "I felt frustrated and felt like looking for sex all over again." This is because the most important factor is missing. While a man might fantasise about getting great satisfaction from a woman he is paying, which is what his mind tells him, the missing connection causes feelings of emptiness and dissatisfaction in the long run. With paid sex, the woman is not 'present'. By hiring out her vagina, she disconnects from herself emotionally; otherwise, she couldn't perform that service with such frequency.

Connection with our partners gives us feelings of belonging and a sense of sharing, caring, and being loved, which we all seek. Without it, we feel empty, lost, and alone. Connection is a feeling we all need; it sustains us, and it's what makes us feel alive; it keeps us healthy and connected to life! Even animals need nurturing; without it, they die. A baby elephant will die without nurturing from its mother.

One of the cases I read when I was studying psychology, was a study done on baby monkeys in three separate cages. One had a branch covered with fur, and the monkey grew up relatively normal. The other monkey had a branch with no fur, and it withdrew from playfulness. The third monkey had no branch, only a concrete cage; it became sickly and did not survive. These are simple examples of how lack of connection affects behaviour with primates and has even more variations for us humans.

The Golden Key to Sexual Prowess Is Your 'Being Energy'

The reason we say I'm *being* in love, I'm *being* on a holiday, or I'm *being* with a friend or in an art gallery is because we experience this through our hearts, the 'being' part of us.

Another way to tell the difference between being in the heart or your mind is; think about when you are having sex. Again, you are not *doing* sex; you are having an experience by *being* in your body and being with someone. You are not thinking in the middle of it (hopefully); you are just *being* there, enjoying it. The same way we go out to the theatre or to a movie, we want to enjoy without thinking; we are therefore participating by 'being' present.

If you are wondering what you are doing then you need to ask yourself why you are in this situation. When you are questioning rather than participating, you are stepping out from 'being present' and enjoying the moment; this is an important fact to ponder! Consider being on holiday and relaxing. Or take for example, when you're planning anything going on a holiday or even going on a short trip. At these times you are actively connecting to the 'being' part of you. We need these breaks to get in touch with the being part of us as it is this energy within, that heals and balances us internally.

To Conclude: You can experience a joyful, exhilarating experience and maintain this connection outside sexual intercourse. This happens with sports, dancing, and other activities, which ultimately have a calming effect on your body and considerably reduce tiredness and stress. Joyful activities have an uplifting effect on the body mechanism by not just increasing your energy level but re-balancing your entire system.

Connection is the Key

The main reason pornography does not fulfil males in the long run is that it's about the mind. It's a visual experience with no connection to the being state that resides within the heart. It ends up only irritating and frustrating in the long run, similar to the exasperation and frustration commonly felt at the end of a losing in a gambling session. Good reference here is in the movie:- "Going for Broke", see how you identify with it.

Connection is the key. You can think all day, plan all day, look at pictures all day for months on end, but if you are not connecting with your heart, you will not get the balance that comes from joy, which is the being state, because you are still in your mind.

The reason people love watching weddings is that they are all about the being state the connection to your heart that connects you with joy. A massage or a Reiki healing will give you that same feeling of connection.

From this wholeness comes balance that promotes fulfilment; it's the reason we all strive to fulfil our dreams. This important connection is what we all seek from family life; through our families we connect to the being state within ourselves. It's not something we can conjure up, it's not connected to thinking; it's about the feeling within the heart itself.

An example is people who get involved with charities or help others in various ways, especially in the personal development field with the many courses available. Such courses and charity work are all about connection; people really need to connect with other people, which helps them connect with themselves.

The more connected we are with ourselves, the more we can assist others and offer a higher level of service. People for example who run personal development sessions have usually had breakthroughs of some sort and have developed an understanding within themselves first. Therefore, those who pay top dollar for these courses actually take advantage of fast track learning and understanding on how to attain that next level whether its in business, wealth creation, or personal relationships; and be happier which is the aim of us all. The being state is this 'missing link' to our internal power source and true happiness that we all seek through the many areas of our lives.

Switching on Your "Being State" Exercise

Sit comfortably and recline your head, totally immersing yourself in a nice, physical sensation residing in your body allowing yourself to feel your body relaxing on the inside and breathing in that wonderful, relaxed feeling. Breathe it in for two to three minutes so you can feel you are enjoying breathing in and resting in a nice pleasant feeling. At this very moment you are feeling, not thinking of anything at all.

As you are doing this, bring into your consciousness someone you love and who loves you or a pleasant experience you may have had, and feel yourself breathing in that delightful feeling, filling up and expanding into this original feeling. Let yourself enjoy the feeling as you are doing it. Next, bring into your mind something you really enjoy doing, like a special place you visit, a recent holiday, or hobby, a recent party, or something that gives you that pleasurable relaxed feeling. Breathe this feeling in a few times, topping up on what is already there. As you relax more, tell yourself how lucky you are to have people in your life who love you, to be living where you live, and to be able to do what you do with your gifts and talents. You are effectively building a strong energy that is recharging your body with positive, revitalizing energy.

Make a note where in your body you are feeling this energy while doing this exercise. Bring to mind a time when someone may have appreciated you, or acknowledged you, or touched you in some way that made you feel special and connect to this feeling. We can forget to be grateful and acknowledge what we have to be grateful for! We should feel how lucky we are with those of us living in Australia or another peaceful location; having good incomes and good food, being looked after and privileged, having families and sunshine and enjoyable lives, and being of sound body and mind. We have much to be thankful for, but we generally forget to be grateful for these simple things we take for granted. We don't need to focus on negative images or what we don't have; we should focus on what we do have!

Creating a Magic Image File

Now that you have experienced this energy inside your body, did you notice where in your body the feeling was? You could start with feeling your feet or shoulders relaxing first. This might happen especially if one part of your body has been aching or is more tired than another part. If this is you, let that part relax first by breathing some breaths into it. Then allow your chest to relax until you can feel the relaxation around your heart centre area. Now decide to make an attachment, or file, of this wonderful visualization so you can open it at any time.

Give this file a name, like 'sitting in a forest' or 'sitting on a cloud' or 'sun baking by the sea side'. Now close the file. Sit up, shifting your position from the reclining one you were in, and open your eyes, and think of something you dislike, which could be something that happens on a daily basis you don't have control over. Make an intention and decide which feeling you prefer—right now!

Having decided, go back to the reclining position and sink straight back into the nice strengthening feeling you were just in. Recognize how easy it is to choose. Yes, that is effectively what just occurred—you made a choice! If you can remember this, all you ever need to do is *choose*; you will always have better control over your energy rather than feeling a victim of circumstances.

Simply by changing position, focusing on a positive, associating the nice feeling that comes with it, and allowing yourself to enjoy it, you can change your 'state' or mood every time! Now that you have this wonderful feeling at your beck and call, how would you like to start every day feeling this way, just by bringing this feeling into your body and breathing it in? Good decision?

Having made this decision, open your eyes, and on the movie screen of your mind, picture your future self-getting into a car. While it's warming up, recline your head on the headrest and open your file. Breathe in the relaxation and positivity of the delightful feeling through your body now, washing off all that tired negative stuff and filling yourself up with that feel-good, light energy!

The most effective way to have this energy become your new default energy is to do this for a few minutes first thing in the morning and a few times during your day. That way you can refresh yourself by simply taking in a few deep breaths of a delightful energizing feeling, surrounding yourself and filling yourself up with it. Standing by an open window or consciously breathing in fresh air on a short walk will do it also.

To Conclude: Connecting to a relaxation feeling in your body is the being state, which is breathing in and holding onto pleasurable feelings that can be about anything. This is different from the images that come from our minds; they are the visual experiences our minds produce, whereas pleasurable experiences are connected with emotions, our 'being state'.

Understanding the Chakras: Your Energy Centres

By consciously integrating and balancing your energy through your chakras, you can create that nice feeling of wholeness in your physical body and harmony in your emotional life. Balancing your chakras integrates your mental attitude and strengthens your emotions. The chakras are part of the way we think and feel; they are the energy centres that interact with our bodies' sensations. Balanced chakras mean balanced lives.

Blocked energy is a result of stress that produces symptoms such as fear, nausea, tiredness, and anxiety, among others. *Blocked energy is the cause, and left unchecked, it can gradually develop into physical symptoms, including a depletion of sexual power.*

Creativity and sexuality come from the same chakra. When our emotions are blocked, chances are one or more chakras are blocked. Blocked chakras will gradually bring our energy down. (See http://www.healer.ch/Chakras-e.html.)

Each centre has a specific function. When all centres are aligned with positive energy, we experience vibrancy and joy. If you look closely at the chakra system, you will see that the energy centres interact with your emotional states. This means your emotional state influences how your chakras keep your body vibrant. When you are feeling down, your mood has an effect on your chakras specific to the feelings you are experiencing. You can raise uplift your energy through the chakras by increasing your 'feel good' feelings.

Focusing and breathing into each chakra is like revving the engine to warm up a car. In this way, you can raise the energy within the chakras by simply focusing on your breath alone. Using the simple exercise mentioned above in creating a 'magic file' will stimulate, expand, and spread your energy throughout your body, and you can begin to control your energy. There is one particular CD that will teach you how to do this very easily releasing stress at the same time called: "Balance your Mind' Go to : http://www.essentiallifeskills.com/online_shop.html.

The Chakra System: The Psychic Energy Centres in Your Body

The **base chakra** is tied to our survival instincts, our fight-or-flight response that causes us to run away if in a fearful situation or stand and fight. This centre, our grounding part, governs our need to settle down when we have found partners. It is the focus of the Kundalini or 'serpent power' in yoga terms, where our sexual energy resides.

The **sacral centre** is the place from where our creative energy flows or is suppressed. All our potential creative energy resides within this chakra. This centre comes into play when we imagine materializing our ideas. Hence, a baby grows and is nurtured in this region.

The **solar plexus chakra** is our power centre. When people are hunching over, they are usually protecting their power centres, and they will say, "He makes me sick to my stomach." It's a reaction to feeling powerless. This centre is also responsible for the feeling of "butterflies," dread, anxiety, etc., many feelings we have and react to, perceiving them as coming from the outside.

At the opposite end, our feelings of excitement and pride come from this chakra. Feelings of reward for something we did well come from this centre.

The **heart chakra** is the flower that closes when we have been hurt or suffer what we perceive as hurt. The broken-heart syndrome is when the chakra closes somewhat. Then, when a friend takes us for a drink or lunch, we get the "Oh, I feel a lot better" feeling, until again we remember how our poor heart is suffering, and back comes the feeling. It's also through the heart that we feel appreciation, gratitude, and warmth toward others, and it's in this centre that we feel the warmth of a nice atmosphere or company. *It's a feeling we respond to rather than react to.*

The feeling of gratitude and appreciation ignites the heart chakra, the body's main power centre and the activator of our immunity systems. When we share our feelings, we feel more deeply connected to our essential energy. Love rejuvenates our whole system; it literally ignites the cells throughout our bodies. The heart is the main power source, and the solar plexus is a power centre, but not the power source. When we say a bride "glows" on her wedding day, it's because of the activation of the heart centre, the power source that radiates this extra energy.

The **throat chakra** is the centre through which we voice our truths, stand up for ourselves, and stand in our power. When circumstances prevent us from expressing the truth, we may begin to suppress our voices and energy. This gradually leads to suppressing our immune systems, and we will "catch whatever is going around." This is merely a cop-out, a denial of what we are feeling or suppressing. Over time, suppressed energy leads to disease in the body and manifests as the flu or worse. By speaking our truth, our energy slowly returns, giving us the feeling of being conquerors and owning the stages of our lives' challenges.

Have you ever noticed in movies how the mafia characters do not have clear voices, but very hoarse voices instead; their truth is so suppressed that they can barely speak clearly. You can recognise a lot from a person by the clarity of their voice.

The **brow chakra** is the seat of intuition from where all our dreams and goals originate. Looking to our futures comes from the brow chakra. The planning part follows the intuitive part and does not precede it, as planning comes from our minds. It's from this centre that we sense future events concerning others or ourselves. Confusion and indecision cause congestion in this chakra, and headaches can develop as a result. Unresolved issues and when situations back up and are un-dealt with, will frequently leads to migraine headaches.

The **crown chakra** is our connection with central intelligence, our inner wisdom. The more a person meditates, the clearer and more connected he or she comes to the truth that governs his or her life and to the wisdom of sustainable health and longevity. This is generally blocked when people choose to go against their inner wisdom or gradually disown their truths or shut down from love. This chakra will gradually shut down altogether when a person turns to crime. This happens gradually; hence, a tough or cold expression on a person's face indicates how shut down or open that individual has become.

The journey of finding your inner truth is arduous. As people and religions generally cannot quantify God, 'central intelligence' is a simple way of getting a clear understanding of this higher aspect of ourselves, which controls our heartbeat and regulates hair growth and governs the aging process in our bodies. It also miraculously heals our bodies, and conducts the childbirth process. All these functions are connected with this part of us, which controls the whole body mechanism, hence the term 'central intelligence'. It's a wise decision to get more in touch with this divine aspect within yourself that conducts your life unseen to you!

Central Intelligence Defined

Your energy source is your unlimited power. People generally pay lip service to this and associate power to movies, guns, and business, but discipline is rarely mentioned. Actual power lies within, but it needs discipline to grow and nurture. Like an undisciplined child who creates havoc, so does energy when you are not in control of it. A fire can be channeled to produce heat warmth and cook and iron your clothes or grow out of control and create havoc on so many levels; in the same way so can your energy cause grief or healing depending on how you use it.

The reason people generally do not understand themselves is that most have no concept of this higher self or aspect of central intelligence, or God source that every human has within them. This is our energy running through us, it's the energy that causes us to breathe, it's the energy inside you that causes your biological clock to be on time with aging and healing and processing food and eliminating waste from your body. It's the energy within you that allows you to feel and connect with and understand others, people and nature around you. To acknowledge this energy means you need to stop, recognize, consider, be grateful, be helpful, share and care more, be open, and recognize you are an eternal living soul. That you inhabit your body and at night this very central intelligence causes renewal to happen magically, so that when you awaken you feel refreshed something we all take for granted and never stop to wonder how that may actually work.

However, with so many beliefs in our world today, we have to make individual journeys to find our truths by our own paths, which are covered with many pitfalls. In the long run it strengthens us to find our own path, but in the short term it frustrates and keeps us in the dark, so we get lost and feel lonely and search most of our lives to find this elusive part, (that we generally seek in the other person i.e. soul mate) When and if we do find this part, we discover that it has been waiting patiently for us to stop, listen, breathe, and be grateful for being part of life's ever-changing beauty and order that resides peacefully within us.

The majesty of discovering this illusive higher self or central intelligence is generally stumbled upon by people either under severe crisis who are at deaths door or have crossed over and had a "pre- death experience" and actually caught a glimpse of the other side with all its grandeur and majestic inexplicable beauty and peace. As was portrayed in a TV program with individuals recounting their experiences after being pronounced dead either on the operating table or in a car accident. A program called: "I Survived Beyond and Back".

Also in her book "Dying to be Me" now translated into 28 languages, Anita Moorjani told how she returned 'from the other side', to heal after a horrendous illness that took more than 5 years of her life. When she had an epiphany of what was behind her illness, it enabled her to have a miraculous recovery that stunned the doctors worldwide.

For the vast majority of people however this part of us can easily be glimpsed through meditation and through higher sexual experiences as the next levels to sex, when one connects to the ecstatic realms; which generally happens when the persons heart is open and they are free to love and be loved. Some of this is taught in advanced Tantra.

Hence Aleister Crowley wanted to explore this realm, however love and pleasure cannot be forced nor exploited and pleasure of the body is limited to the body. Hence to experience ecstatic realms one needs to be connected with the divine within, which is accessible only though love which was the reason why Aleister Crowley could not get there as he was experimenting through pleasure and control, with no knowledge of the important role that love plays in pursuing divine consciousness. This is why love is the highest power of all and overcomes all, and is equal in the same way in both sexes, where as Aleister Crowley considered women to be inferior to men.

For this reason all-healing is achievable through the gateway of love and acceptance within, which is our **Internal Central Intelligence**. Connect with this and you will always stay balanced and healthy, this is the key for peace, health and longevity.

Using your Sexual Energy as Healing Energy "Exercise"

Feel the warmth of your hands. Move that warmth by placing your hands on your belly. Feel the warmth until you can put your hands on any part of your body and create a warm, comforting feeling. "See" yourself as an energy source, and continue, 'seeing' this energy as though you were connecting to the sun or standing in a beam of light. This visual image is an easy way to maintain a connection to the energy source, or light beam. Opening and closing your eyes while doing this will give you a greater sense that this energy is present inside as well as outside you. Don't rush it. Your energy is something you feel, not see with your physical eyes, so don't try to 'see' it initially.

Feel how you want to connect to a loving or caring feeling inside yourself. It's the same feeling you might have for someone you love. Alternatively, you can focus on how holding your favourite pet makes you feel, or being on a recent holiday, or just walking along the beach or in the bush. Gently stroke your tummy as you feel this energy. This is generally referred to as 'healing energy'. It's what mothers and lovers use all the time when holding a child or a loved one.

"Easy Exercise" Healing Pain in the Body

We can 'see' how feelings are connected to touch and how frequently we deny ourselves this touch, hence our need to be touched by others. Do this little touch exercise frequently: touch your arm, stroke your hand against your belly or heart, repeating, "I am a gentle, loving person," and just see how this feels and how these words affect you. This is something you cannot rush; expressing love is not something you can rush for yourself or for another.

At this point, you may be associating forgotten images from your childhood. Allow the tears to come up, and if they do, let yourself feel whatever comes up by simply breathing into the feeling. This is a healing process far more effective than any medicine. Continue the gentle stroking over the possible emotional pain or hurt that may be associated with some part of your body.

Doing this process repeatedly, will gradually release-blocked energy, which is what is normally responsible for pain that you may feel in parts of your body. The answer to the pain is all tied up within the nerves and muscles, and a simple way of accessing the reason for your pain is by patiently and repeatedly practising the exercise described here. By simply following this method described here, you can access the answers behind the pain that may have been there for years. See *Healing Inner Child,* at : http://www.essentiallifeskills.com/online_shop.html. This CD will enable you to follow and do the necessary process by guiding you though healing step by step gently and effectively.

Introducing the Six-Step Healing Exercise

This six-step exercise is like connecting up your computer. Until you connect your computer to the Internet, you have only partial benefit. So be connected to this exercise; maintain the connection and it will enable you to feel the power and benefit of this technique. Until you make that connection, you will not experience the magic feeling you can get from the exercise on a daily basis. Patience is the key. Once you have made the connection, it's straightforward after that.

In the beginning, focus on moving the energy from the stomach to the solar plexus area; using one hand, gently stroke the stomach in an upward direction. The idea is to direct your energy from the tummy, where your hands start warming you, up until this energy slowly travels to the crown of your head. As one hand is gently stroking the sexual area energy upward, the other hand is gently stroking the tummy region in the same way. You should look like you are strumming a guitar. You are focusing on moving the energy up; you will feel a delightful sexual energy rippling through your body.

As you stay present to that energy, avoid the urge to climax or associating it to a sexual orgasm. Just see if you can feel it as your own energy rather than trying to connect it to sex. It's quite wonderful when you discover you can do something like immersing yourself in your energized feeling and feel great while doing it. Try it!

The Six Steps

The first three steps create a path:

Step 1. As you are gently stroking your genital area, you are breathing in and exhaling as your hand reaches your tummy. Do this with gentle, repeated stokes, alternating hands, slowly directing the stroking massage in a straight line upward along the stomach and stopping at the solar plexus. Repeat twice.

Step 2. Repeat the first step, only this time, when your hands reach your belly, inhale and hold your breath until your hands reach the solar plexus. Exhale with a medium deep breath. Repeat twice.

Step 3. Place your left hand on your solar plexus, creating a warm sensation on your tummy. With your right hand, gently stroke the same way upward along your belly, inhaling as you pass the belly button. The right hand now delivers the energy you have been stroking upward into your cupped left hand on your tummy, as though the left were a letterbox waiting for a letter to be delivered. Once the right hand has brought that energy to the cupped left hand, it returns to the position on the solar plexus as you exhale lowering the right hand. Repeat twice.

Step 4. To stroke the energy up, the fourth step requires both hands to be moving upward. While the left hand stays gently on the sexual area, the right hand now strokes this energy up as though dragging and caressing it toward the tummy region. The hands gently caress up toward the solar plexus, and you again inhale at the belly.

Repeat this several times until you get the sensation that the energy is moving a little toward the solar plexus, even if it's just a slight feeling.

On reaching the solar plexus, make an audible *ahhhhh* sound on the exhalation. This will make it more real and will enable you to feel 'the connection' to your energy (as an example of your computer connecting to your server). The hand movements without the *ahhhhh* sound can be compared to working on computer without a network connection.

Step 5. Repeat step 4, saying *ahhhhh* and stroking your tummy. Then, with the exhaling breath, bring your hands upward, touching your throat and feeling the humming *mmmmm* sound you now make when your hands rest on your throat. When you make the *ahhhhh* sound while you stroke your body, you get the sensation of it into your body easier, and it stops your mind from engaging in the judgement game.

Step 6. This step is what I call "the cherry on top." At this point, you are gently massaging your genitals with one hand and your crown with the other. By now, the energy has spread to the top of your head. This feels like a warm buzz spreading through your body. You have activated your sexual "wow" factor energy. Don't be too disappointed if you don't achieve this feeling the first or second time. The object here is to gather this energy, so don't rush it. It's not a conquest; it's wonderful buzzing feeling that energizes you the more you do it.

The top-up. By using this final step, you can give yourself an energy boost anytime simply because you have opened up the 'link' to this energy. If you start the energy up before you start work in the morning, your body will readily respond when you reconnect or 'top up' on that lovely feeling anytime throughout your day. You can repeat the 'top up' step as many times during the day as you wish, and it can be done as simply as taking a breath over a cuppa or giving your tummy a gentle rub that will boost your mood as well. If you didn't initiate these steps in the morning, it may be a bit hard to do because your mind won't be in gear to link your energy to the visualization part of the exercise.

Don't forget that your mind is your tool, it's not who you are. You can be sure of this, because we say, "My mind, my body." We don't say, "I mind" or "I body."

Overcoming Your Mind

"But my mind gets in the way of me feeling good" is a common response, and here's why: the mind communicates to us with images. For example, if you were to think of what your car looks like or what you had for breakfast or what ice cream tastes like, an image immediately pops up. That's when you're in your mind, but there are times when you're in your body. When you're engaged in judgement, criticism, analysis, or assessment, you're in your mind; during sex, you're in your body, not your mind, so you don't generally think things such as "When was it better?" or "How did I do that...?"

The best way of 'overcoming' your mind is by becoming aware of what you are doing first, then you can identify the interference of the ever-chattering mind. Exercise distracts the mind, giving you an insight to its constant chatter. You may have been unaware of this. Most of the ongoing mind stuff is images being processed with comments you have allowed to go on. You can control this negative chatter by recognizing it's there and deciding to say no to the "stuff" it's churning out.

When you begin to do this seriously and with some discipline, your mind will become your very useful tool, prompting you with reminders and acknowledgements rather than criticisms and negative self-talk. Many accumulated images are references to negative experiences that have become part of your memory- bank references the same way as nice images from a holiday are also part of your internal references. Your mind does not discriminate and will bring up images associated with whatever emotion is present at the time. This is where awareness comes in, being mindful and recognising an image from a past event and simply saying no in the same way you would say no at a restaurant to something you did not order. It is just as necessary to say no emphatically to random negative images that pop up in your mind for no apparent reason.

To Conclude: When your emotions are blocked, chances are one or more of the chakras are blocked. Pain is a symptom of blocked chakras, which will gradually bring your energy down. Using these specialized exercises will unblock negative energy from the chakras, providing you do the exercises at regular intervals. It's important to stop the mind chatter that incessantly reminds you of past negative associations. Staying aware is the key to dismissing mind chatter rather than taking it on as though it were real.

Understanding the Principles of Your Mind

Understanding the principles behind your mind gives you an objective sense of how the mind comes into play and how to work with your energy and stay focused on any exercise rather than being distracted by your mind. The mind analogy below gives a good way to remember the difference so you can identify how mind-control works.

1. Mind = Charioteer
2. Emotions = Reins
3. Senses = Horses
4. Soul = Passenger
5. Body = Chariot

When the charioteer (the mind) is in control of the reins (the emotions), the horses (the senses) can be driven in an orderly fashion so the passenger (the soul) can reach a destination safely and the chariot (the body) can stay undamaged.

However, when the mind (the charioteer) loses control of emotions (the reins), the senses (the horses) cannot be controlled and run amuck, ending up in a ditch or over a cliff, damaging the chariot (the body) and preventing the passenger (the soul) from reaching a destination.

These principles come from ancient scriptures and have been used through the ages, by trying to remember how the mind works using these principles will serve you throughout your life, if you remember to apply them.

How Sexual Energy is Transferred with Multiple Partners

The analogy of the mind is a very important analogy to keep in mind because we also forget that most of what we eat is to satisfy the sense of taste. Very few of us remember that unless we consider the importance of nourishing our bodies, they will seize up in exactly the same way as putting a mixture of water and oil into the petrol tank, which you would never do would you? Our "petrol tanks" can be likened to our minds, yet we fill them with all kinds of "rubbish." No wonder we don't feel well.

Just as petrol is in the fuel tank, our pure energy is at the base of the spine and connected to the sexual energy. We have labelled our pure energy as sexual energy, not realizing this is the seat or main switch to our power. We can harness this power and use it as energy not just for sex. This is generally because we don't understand how this energy can be channelled and prolonged instead of wasted. When we are not in charge of our sexual energy and when we absorb other people's 'negative energy residue' through indiscriminate sex, this is the typical example of putting rubbish into the petrol tank.

The petrol tank analogy is a good way to see indiscriminate sex e.g. intimacy = into me see. When you are having sex with several partners, their energy transmits into your energy centres, so whatever those partners are going through in their lives—turmoil, trauma, hang-ups, confusion, grief, guilt, unresolved anger, resentment—you will be affected by it more and more the longer you stay with them. It gets transmitted to you in larger doses if you are in the habit of indulging in this activity.

These individuals may comment that they feel disoriented and not in the best moods, as a lot of that energy has been siphoned into them, and they generally don't realize that the feeling of being 'out of it' is a direct result of this type of negative energy transferred directly into their chakra systems.

You can learn how to use sexual energy in its many forms through techniques obtainable on the site below. They give males longer staying power and increase their energy daily. Practicing these methods regularly gives them total control of their orgasms, as the energy flows easier and they no longer feel tired or drained after sex as a result balancing your energy with this easy method. (See www.theorgasmiceffect.com.)

Our Power Source—The Healing Power Inside

We are all connected to the power source within us through our Kundalini centre, situated at the base chakra, but only a very small percentage of us know how to maintain this connection on a conscious level, and most of us are not consciously connected. We refer to this "awesome" source by names such as God, when we are not consciously connected and when our awareness is still on the subconscious level.

The power source is present in us all. We can call it the God factor or inner power. I refer to this as central intelligence. The way to discover that it is actually present within you is to ask yourself the question; who is healing my body when it's recovering from a broken bone or an operation or a simple thing such as a cut on your skin. Do you know how to do that healing, do you know how to mend broken bones or cuts inside you? The obvious answer is No. We do not have a clue how that is being done on the inside; it's our internal central intelligence that is automatically mending and healing us without our knowledge.

So the question that follows here is, if animals heal, does this mean they have central intelligence also? Yes, of course they do. The only difference is we have soul consciousness, whereas the animals have simple consciousness and have a group soul rather than individual souls as we do. This means that animals have many bodies per group soul. This is discussed at length in C. W. Leadbeater's book *Textbook of Theosophy 1912*. He isn't the only one to discover this information; however, he explains it in simple terms. This information comes from very ancient texts called the Vedas or Vedanta, which precede the

Christian era by thousands of years. (See http://www.cwlworld.info/html/books.html.)

Exercise: Plug into Your Internal Power and Release Stress Fast

Do this little exercise before sleep or before an important meeting or any challenging situation; it takes only about ten minutes. You can do this lying down or sitting comfortably.

Step 1. Start with relaxing yourself. Next, see yourself as a hollow glass container filling up with a brilliant- coloured liquid. See this brilliant colour fill your body, from your feet to the top of your head. Place your left hand on top of your head and see this as the "tap" through which the coloured liquid flows. Place your right hand on your heart. This way you will be more consciously connected to what you are doing and not as easily distracted by your wandering mind.

Step 2. As the brilliant coloured liquid fills your body, "see" it slowly filling up at your feet and ankles, knees, and thighs. See this brilliant colour rising to the level of your stomach, then your diaphragm, and now your lungs, "breathing" this brilliant colour in and watching as this colour fills your heart and lungs area, arms, and all the way up to the crown of your head. By the time it reaches your head, you will get a sense of what colour this "liquid" is that's filling you.

Step 3. You might want to do this several times, each time bringing to mind either a holiday you focus on while breathing in and filling up on a peaceful feeling, as the colour fills you, or imagining yourself floating on a cloud or a lake, lagoon, or ocean.

Step 4. Stay focused for as long as possible and not fall asleep so your body can consciously relax that way. This will allow you to fall into relaxed sleep or clear your mind of tension and relax your body in the process. Either way is a win-win situation.

Protection Technique

This powerful exercise protects you from people's negative energy. This is another way you can use your chakras and aura as protection, protecting your energy from other people's negativity, which could be draining you in your daily life.

If you are going to visit someone in the hospital or visit relatives who "press your buttons," then doing this protection exercise will slowly counteract the negative effect or energy drain you usually feel in their presence. For greater protection, do the 'filling up' on the brilliant colour several times. When the colour reaches your crown the second and third time around, focus on that colour being gold and as you continue seeing the gold white light within you, surround that with an aqua turquoise colour all around the gold colour. This will make you feel more relaxed and at peace with yourself.

Aqua turquoise is a healing colour; we know this because nature is green and the sky is blue, and when we sit outdoors for a while, we feel energized in about twenty minutes or so. Plants grow better outdoors than indoors even if they're near an open window. We don't really know how this works—we just call it nature; I like to call it Akasha which according to the Samkhya school of Hindu philosophy, Akasha is one of the five <u>Mahābhūtas</u> (grand physical elements) having the specific property of sound, which is the universal energy force. Filling yourself up on the colour of nature will give you the same effect. Just try it every time you feel a little down on your energy, and you will see how it totally changes your mood. All you need is a little trust in the process, and you will see how it works every time.

If you sit for ten minutes in the morning just inhaling and taking your time to breathe and nothing else, you will see how energizing this will be at the start of each day. This is an excellent and easy method to guide you into relaxing breathing experience to have at your fingertips that you can access anytime. You can get this directly at : http://www.essentiallifeskills.com/shop/balance-your-mind-cd.htm

For extra protection against people with negative energy, having filled up on the turquoise and gold colour, put purple around the gold and aqua. By surrounding yourself with purple on the outside of the aqua, will strengthen the whole protection bubble you will see yourself sitting inside. It's not necessary to 'see' the colour as long as you can visualize it. Here's why: If someone asked you the colour of your front door or your car, you wouldn't be able to see it, but you wouldn't have any trouble visualizing it, would you? The same applies here. As long as you get some image, that is all that matters. It works because you start to focus.

When you have practiced this several times over a period of say, a month or more, you will easily be able to top up on this relaxing protective energy during the day or when you need extra energy. What's more, you will be very surprised how well it works, and you will want to do this more often because of its beneficial effects. Each time, you will find it easier to do. You will notice the difference in the way you feel when you have done the exercise and when you have not. When problems arise on the days when you *have* done the exercises, you will feel so much more relaxed about them than you normally would. On days you don't do the exercise, you'll feel the usual flustered or rushed state that you are familiar with. It's a pleasant change to feel the easy control with such little effort.

Feelings are connected to touch, and we frequently deny ourselves touch, hence our need to be touched by others.

Mastering Energy Control

Have you ever noticed that 'whatever you focus your mind' on is somehow drawn to you? For example, if you are particularly afraid of spiders and keep focusing on this, you will materialize this and somehow they will 'seem to' appear from nowhere. How does that work? Another example is the insurance guy who tries to get you to focus upon your worst fear to sell you a policy.

You may recall a familiar experience when you wondered, "How did that happen?" When you really think about the event, however, you'll see how focusing on certain thoughts somehow plays the situation into reality.

Here are more examples:

1. Following skydiving, the people who landed in trees were asked what they were thinking about seconds before they jumped. Those who feared an accident had one, while those who were excited and thought of something pleasant didn't. Some focused on hoping they wouldn't land in trees, but by focusing on what they didn't want, they focused on that very thing, so they landed in trees. That's a direct example of how focusing works: focus on what you want, not what you don't want.

2. At a restaurant, do you tell the waiter everything you *don't* like? No. You order what you *do* like and expect it to come to you. It's the same here: whatever you focus on becomes an order you're making; you draw it to you, seemingly like magic. Except it's not magic, it's one of the laws that govern us, the law of attraction.

How to Get What You Truly Desire

Start by visualizing your dreams. How do you want to spend the next three to five years? What do you see yourself doing? In your heart of hearts, what do you want to be, do, and have? *Make a mental picture.* Focus on an image, one you *really* want. Is it a great relationship? Is it being financially well off? Is it a great home or lifestyle? A nice car or be a better lover?

It's all about the decision to move forward; once made, the rest follows. It's like learning to play tennis or ride a motorbike—you are only as good as your practice.

Some people want to improve their careers or health or relationships or even their golf games. Whatever it is, make this your daily affirmation and focus. Write down or draw a picture of what you want, a short- or long-term outcome. Unless you write it down, it will slip by and be taken over by the momentum of that day or week. If you don't write it down, it may come up later but will feel harder to reach. Writing it down gives you that reminder and confirms the dream that you can gradually build on, and this slowly draws it to you.

The techniques in this book are obtainable in several formats via e-book or in a more comprehensive downloadable video in which I present many tips and explain each technique, each of which takes only a few minutes of practice per day to obtain results.

Males can additionally learn how they can last a minimum of twenty minutes in the bedroom every time; it's a life changing method. There are also techniques on how to please a woman, how to be a great lover and have a great relationship too.

See : www.theorgasmiceffect.com

A Tip for the Secret to Success

Now that you have written your desired intention, you have effectively installed a program in your mind much as you would install a program in your computer. Running your new program in your mind several times a day over a month will bring you the success you have imagined. By focusing in this way, you are creating a new habit. We all struggle with our minds; getting the habit to work effectively takes approximately twenty-eight days, after which it will be, your new default response. Doing this daily will remind you that you want to bring this new way of thinking into your mind. Remember, you can do this with anything you wish to have, be, or do. But you do need to keep it up just like you would with anything you practice when you want your results to be on going.

Your mind is your tool, and by disciplining your mind, you can create anything you wish. Most people's troubles are due to lack of discipline, as the mind is generally lazy and causes people to stay stuck in situations. Staying stuck gradually saps your enthusiasm and your energy, until people start believing that it's their fate or that this is way its meant to be, which of course is not true. Some people make things happen, others watch this happen and some wonder…what happened..? Which one are you?

Negative Habits or Thoughts Are Like Weeds

Negative habits or thoughts are like weeds; they do not go away by themselves. We need to pull them out, and the same applies to negative thoughts. Once you become aware of a dysfunctional part of your behaviour that may be running your life, you will eventually want to get rid of it or perhaps simply switch it off. It's very simple; when you decide to apply yourself and do this each time, old familiar, negative thought patterns will stop coming up.

A negative thought is enough to trigger a replay of a familiar thought quite unconsciously. It's a bit like a computer virus; as soon as you've identified it, you can do something about it. It's the same with disempowering feelings; as soon as they get a hold on you, you can "step out" of them before, they drag you down. By simply saying 'no' to a negative thought each time it comes up is how you get control. It's just a thought, so you can say no to it, but first you need to acknowledge it. You cannot change what you can't acknowledge.

Best way to identify negative energy is to see it as weeds that can return at any moment. Energy blockages are the same, so eliminating them requires vigilant awareness of the underlying, persistent, negative self-talk. Negative self-talk will go on all the time if you let it. Ridding yourself of negative self- talk is a matter of remembering to say 'no' every time it comes up and never letting up your vigilance!

How to Free Yourself of Negative Programs

You can break down negative programs. They are there because you have let them in and allowed them to overstay their welcome, like viruses in a computer. Uninstalling viruses from the mind (i.e. the human computer) is simply being aware of what habitually comes into your mind automatically, without you really thinking and recognizing that your habit has become an ingrained program.

Saying no when you become aware of a negative thought trains your mind to recognize that this habitual thought is no longer welcome. In Phyllis Krystal's book 'Taming the Monkey Mind', she explains how your mind can be likened to a monkey you can never catch because it's always running away and interrupting everything you do. The important thing is to 'catch your mind' each time negative thoughts come up.

For some people, turning negative thoughts around will take time. The key to catching disempowering thoughts is vigilance in recognizing what may be coming from a time when negative thoughts told you what you couldn't do. When you catch them going down this familiar negative track, try to recognize a familiar voice, and then ask yourself if you really want to continue listening to it. Learning to say no to that noise in your head is a matter of recognizing the feeling you don't want to hear or feel anymore. You need to say no for a minimum of a month to form a new, positive, long-term habit.

I always knew no matter what challenging life situations I was facing; I could always do a variety of physical or mental exercises or meditation that would give me a refreshed feeling. They were my strategies for maintaining a happy, balanced life. This has always helped me stay connected to loving feelings and maintain my youthful body.

When you have created good habits, they will always work for you as long as you consistently maintain them! Applying these laws simplifies every part of your life, but you need to follow them; *they are life's recipes for essential life skills.* Continuously saying no is what gets you to consciously recognize and end your un-resourceful outmoded negative thought patterns, the unwanted stuff that has been renting space in your mind.

The new mindset allows you to have a new reference point, which becomes a new way of perceiving and relating to your world and essentially becomes your new default program, the new you!

Remember, it takes twenty-eight days to implement your new positive habit, which then becomes your new default. And like a garden that constantly needs to be weeded, so too you need to stay vigilant about your past habits, which may creep in when you least suspect them. It's all about focus.

Mind is the Master power that moulds and makes,
And Man is Mind, and evermore he takes
The tool of thought, and, shaping what he wills,
Brings forth a thousand joys, or a thousand ills:—
He thinks in secret, and it comes to pass:
Environment is but his looking-glass.

"As a Man Thinketh"
by James Allen

Healing the Inner Child (found at www.essentiallifeskills.com) or the CD with exercises gives you an easy way to identify and release all your negative habits.

To Conclude: The power within us can be harnessed as energy and used not just for sex. Learning how to use sexual energy in its many forms involves a number of simple techniques. When you discover your body is healed from within and coordinated by your internal central intelligence, you can learn to be more aware of negative thoughts, which are like weeds that block your energy flow and healing power. Creating positive habits and awareness restores and maintains energy flow on all levels and overall wellness to the whole of your mind and body.

Chapter 3

What Do We Mean by
'Sexual Energy'?

Our sexual energy is part of the emotional energy we can activate and enjoy on many levels. As I've already mentioned if we couldn't feel the higher emotions such as gratitude and appreciation, we would feel quite empty; hence, we all crave to feel these emotions, which is one of the reasons for competitive and extreme sports. If no one acknowledged our attainments, we'd find something was missing. Having a family raises all these varied emotions throughout the years. For many of us, these higher emotions are not that easily obtainable, so is it any wonder most people rely on sex as the simplest way of getting pleasant feelings from the only source available to them. Perhaps now better understood.

When We Are Courting

Sex is so much more exciting in the beginning, but apart from the anticipation and novelty of a new partner, sexual activity stimulates all the energy in the body in a positive way, especially when feelings on both sides are honest and real. This is when appreciation and other positive emotions begin to develop on a deeper level.

This appreciation is a feeling experienced in the heart chakra, and in the beginning, we are not consciously aware of this, hence we lose this connection with ourselves later on. We don't realize how it happens on the conscious level in the beginning, and sometimes we want to revive this feeling once again with our partners a few years later but don't know how.

Sexual energy is part of the joy within that has been there since childhood; it's the joy and wonder we all crave. That is why sex is such a turn-on for the vast majority of people. When it happens in a positive relationship, it's part of our creative energy and makes us feel alive.

Sharing these feelings openly enables us to feel more deeply connected with our partners and ourselves. It also gives better and stronger health, joy, relaxation, a sense of adventure, and spontaneity in our lives. Acting wholeheartedly brings our life energy into greater focus and enables us to be more present to everything. When we are wholehearted, our lives are enhanced; we become more creative in other areas of our lives and derive more enjoyment by seeing more opportunities in life. Open-heartedness is the opposite of being closed or shut off. The fact that a particular person is closed is obvious to most people, and withdrawn people usually miss a lot in life.

The key is remembering what you really appreciate, love, and treasure about your partner and expressing that to him or her. It's a feeling we are always searching for and trying to find with other people. The partner search is on again when we lose this wonderful connection, which is an internal feeling. A good tip is to notice while playing with your fun child energy where this feeling is in your body. You will find it's connected to your heart centre, and you may want to get into the habit of engaging your heart with whatever you are doing if you wish to stay balanced and healthy.

How Women Communicate

Women generally love to share compliments and especially advice, so when they have intimate relationships with their men, they want all this same sharing with them. As a result of this ongoing sharing, males get confused and instead think women can be too demanding, and many males get frustrated.

A wife's focus will shift from her husband's needs to those of their growing family. This shift happens slowly, so when her man comes home and places his hand on her bum by way of a greeting, it communicates to her he's in the mood for a quickie. As males generally do not connect with their feelings and may not recognize that their partner's feelings at that moment may be tied up with daily concerns, they will not realize this may irritate her, especially when she does not show it.

Since women benefit from female friendship in numerous ways, such as discussion and ego maintenance, their stress levels are generally lower and their ability to relieve tension seems higher because of this sharing. Sharing their tensions with other women is the reason they are not available for quickies until they have dispersed this tension via some form of communication rather than sexually, as men do. Women want to discuss their days with their man to resolve this ongoing mental activity.

If her loved one were to ask about the highlights of her day to help her unload mentally and emotionally, recognizing she must do so in this manner and not via a quickie, she might comply with his desire for a quickie later. However, if her emotions will be tied up with parenting concerns their relationship could suffer if one or the other does not recognize they must make time for each other and put time aside regularly to maintain long-term harmony.

How Men Communicate

Because males are traditionally the breadwinners, they feel responsible for providing for their families. As a rule, males operate from the rational, logical side of themselves and usually focus on projects at work or home. This usually places considerable demands on them, so males become gradually disconnected from their feelings as a result of mostly operating in their heads, then release stress through their genitals. This common perception among men is the reason they frequently seek this avenue of release by going to adult services rather than discussing these needs with their partners or sharing their intimate feelings with other males.

When males become more involved with family life they continue to feel needed or direct their focus to other areas of life, such as their careers more especially if they feel ostracized by their woman, whose time and attention can be consumed by children. When women unknowingly disconnect from their partners the male in this situation may go looking elsewhere to release his sexual tension.

This can become a problem for most husbands as they experience genuine guilt and hope their wives will not find out, or in some cases, they hope their wives will understand and give them more sexual pleasure. So how do men overcome this cycle? The easiest way to balance their lives is by taking charge of their lives so the build-up does not take over, causing them to resort to the only way they know, adult services.

"Getting Your Rocks Off" a common Expression

When males inadvertently disconnect from their partners they frequently comment on how 'things have lost their meaning' unfortunately, males don't realize that disconnection and stuck-ness are simply energy blockages in their bodies, the major cause of their not lasting longer in the bedroom. As a rule, males seem to be more concerned about their bedroom performance than their emotional and physical blockages.

Males frequently use the expression: "need to get my rocks off" that describes the feeling that all males know very well. Women will never use this phrase, as female energy does not get blocked in the way it does with males, nor do females need to release tension via their genitals as males do.

Because men don't release stress by sharing on various levels among themselves as women do, their pent- up emotion is energy that gradually becomes stuck. Stuck energy is energy that it is not Rowing, hence the expression "getting their rocks off." When energy Rows in a male and he practices the energy-Row method described as the 'orgasmic effect technique', it begins to balance his overall energy and will not accumulate as tension. It's a curious fact that statistics show 75 per cent more men suffer with heart problems and have heart surgery than females do.

Simple Rules for Ladies to Keep Their Men

Ladies, if you want your man to be there for your child's twenty-first birthday or marriage and not start losing interest, staying at the office, or taking long trips, follow these simple rules. Doing so will ensure that he thinks of you and will feel that only you can give him what he needs emotionally and physically, because all men love attention from their women.

An easy, quick way to relax your man after work is simply to give him a refreshing drink when it's practicable or give him a quick foot massage. This will take at most five minutes and will get him out of his head and balance him. It will also give you those five minutes to exchange hellos about each other's days without having to deal with sexual innuendos. The automatic stress that comes from thinking he needs genital release will instead release through this simple means of relaxation. The pressure points on the soles of the feet correspond to the body's organs. This is why foot massages are relaxing for the body.

When your man is already physically stimulated upon arriving home after a long day or stressful work commitments, his physiology by default tells him that further stimulation of his genitals will relax him. In fact, the opposite is true; it simply drains him; every man knows the exhausted feeling after ejaculation. The simple foot massage method will serve in many ways; it doesn't take up a lot of energy or time, and it expresses to your man that loving touch you both may be missing with rushed days. And you will find that this simple gesture works wonders in more ways than one for both of you.

A good idea with the foot massage could be, as you start the massage, you could invite one of the children to take over massaging your partner's feet as you turn your attention to the family meal, or visa- versa which ever is the case. Children love to be involved and will soon recognize who to give the massage to. It's a delight and very cute to feel little gentle hands on your feet and additionally teaches the child to share loving feelings and to recognise a simple way to have mummy or daddy feel better.

What Happens Energetically during Sex for a Male?

As a man usually feels great during sex itself but will generally become disconnected from his partner during the course of the relationship. This causes the male to treat sex as a release from tension. This is why it's important for a male to establish a connection with his partner to feel an emotional connection during sex. When connection becomes absent during sex, this may be okay for a while, but in the long run it means the male is 'practicing' disconnection in other areas of his life as well without realizing it. Furthermore, when disconnection slowly occurs, it leads to enhanced feelings of frustration that lead to anger, despair, and disappointment. This build-up over time then leads to gradually developing health issues in one form or another.

I have observed this during the many years I've treated and advised males on this matter. Emotional energy is part of our energy system and part of our passion. When working at a job that lacks emotional energy and does not offer opportunities to express passion, which happens with doctors and other professionals, the male gets overly tense and may bury his anger by becoming depressed, and then feel withdrawn and defeated, depending on his role models he had while growing up at home as a child.

Emotional drain happens gradually so when a male is not connected to his emotions this pattern will emerge, until he will either become sick or start having moods swings, as repressed anger will surface.

How Disconnection Affects Males in Business

As a male becomes more involved with proving himself in the business world, he may disconnect from his feelings and from himself. In the long term, this causes disconnection in all his relationships, including business relationships. This is why males can lose business deals or friends and, worse, connection with their partners or siblings.

The movie *Pretty Woman*, starring Richard Gere and Julia Roberts, provides a good example of how this unfolds. In it, Edward, the male lead, was so preoccupied with business that he lost sight of how disconnection had created a lack of feeling, leading to hostility in his work relationships; everything became focused on how much he could manoeuvre others for financial gain. As there was nothing more to hold his interest, he lost connection with himself, which led to disconnections in his personal life, hence his need to hire a prostitute, who eventually connected him to his feelings. In one scene, she got him to sit on the grass and take his shoes off. At that point, he began to feel for the first time how it was good just to be alive.

Another movie with a different theme is *The Game*, starring Michael Douglas as a bored multimillionaire disconnected with the people closest to him. His brother, played by Sean Penn, offered to play a game with him. The game challenged him, making him feel alive by presenting a series of life- threatening challenges. The protagonist didn't know it was all part of the game; he thought it was really happening. The game came to a huge climax, when he literally took a leap that threatened his life. The leap was part of the game, orchestrated so he fell safely to the ground, where he was greeted by all the actors who had taken part in 'the game'. He recognized how dead he had become and woke up to participating with life again, all thanks to his brother, whom he was made to believe had died.

The Price We Pay with the Games We Play Unknowingly

Unfortunately, much of life can sometimes become like this game. We tangle ourselves in webs of unnecessary denial, deceit, ignorance, and pain to learn valuable lessons. Many real-life lessons are painful, and like the movie, they involve life-threatening situations because we cannot extricate ourselves from the tangled web we have created. Family dramas or work situations can make some people feel stuck because they cannot get awareness of their energy. They become needlessly involved in another's life drama or get hooked in by another's blame or guilt trip.

Most of us need lessons to experience restriction on an emotional or physical level to learn how to release ourselves and feel free. We can really appreciate freedom by feeling its opposite first. Experiencing restrictions in any situation is a valuable lesson. For example, a doctor I know saw that his hospital was so restrictive with their procedures that it left no room for change. Many doctors could not get to their patients because of so many restrictions. This doctor related to me how they had to work long and unpaid hours to keep up with their demanding workloads. In the end, he had to leave due to accumulated stress and suffered because the system would not budge in spite of people reporting its shortfalls and patients' suffering. When he left, he needed to recover emotionally from all the stress. After a year, he took an amazing job that made use of his talents, and he has become an international leader in his field.

Many challenges come our way disguised as needs to perform, but when we eventually recognize our hearts aren't in them and we step out of the situation, we honour ourselves and recognize that our path is not to suffer or be treated with disrespect. This doctor's example is a good one. Unfortunately, people can take a long time to learn these lessons and learn them only when they are in their fifties or sixties. That's when they realize they have been unnecessarily holding onto misery.

The Lessons Behind Accidents

Unfortunately this disconnection happens to males and females alike. When women are involved in the corporate world working alongside men and take on men roles they become just as disconnected. The competition and analysing that takes over causes women to disconnect from their intuitive abilities and soft natures and become preoccupied with deadlines instead.

When we lose sight of the necessity for relaxation and rush our life instead of making time for relaxation, sometimes life will make us stop forcefully by putting in our way a minor accident to force us to stop and evaluate and rest up. On several occasions I have met people who related to me how a Major Accident they had caused them to recognise they were on the wrong track in their lives. Here is just one example that comes to mind that I thought valuable to mention here of a very unfortunate situation that I was privy to.

Many years ago when I was in my 20ys living in Melbourne and worked in the corporate world there was a young teenager in the office doing work experience. He was a real 'larrikin' who frequently got into mischief including racing his car and showing off. When he left we heard soon after, that he had a major car accident. When I visited him on a few occasions in hospital he was still wired up with tubes going though his throat so he could breathe, his finger nails were totally black from all the drugs that were pumped through his body, and he was pronounced dead three times during the first three months of his ordeal.

Dennis came out of hospital two years later after 16 operations for skin grafts on his leg. When he came out he visited all the people who visited him in the hospital including me. I bumped into him on the street another two years after that, and when he saw me from a distance; he no longer had his walking stick and was jumping around showing me he was all healed. As he walked with a limp beside me, he related how he was grateful for his accident that made him re-think his life. He studied and passed exams while recovering in the hospital. He was now married and had baby on the way, and in his spare time he visited and schools where he was invited to talk about the dangers of speeding on the roads.

To Conclude: Women generally do ego maintenance with shopping and don't use sex to de-stress as men do. Sharing a with a partner or even a friend about the tensions of the day will not only dispel their tension but can bring an opportunity to listen while sharing a drink or a foot massage with the partner. This is such an easy non-intrusive way of reducing tension rather than relying on sexual release to unload that built stress every time.

What is Our Orgasmic Energy ?

Imagine that same sexual energy feeling travelling through your cells, lifting your spirits and revving up your day giving you a feeling of being refreshed. This is the vibrant, raw energy of children that pulsates through their bodies as joy (instead of sexually, as experienced in adult bodies). Its rather a difficult concept to get this after the first time of reading; as energy is not something that scientists can understand nor can it be measured like it can be with their mechanical experiments. Polarization is not something that is generally spoken about unless in mechanical terms hence to understand it thoroughly it does need to be broken down and repeated to appreciate the whole meaning behind how the energy within us actually works.

After about age of eleven, a child's energy becomes polarized, meaning; it divides into rationalising within and, growing sexual development, so they don't begin to interpret and analyse this shifting energy nor does a child ever realize what is really occurring. This polarization marks the beginning of the aging process, where we as individuals slowly separate ourselves from the original joy energy. This is the reason why children usually don't feel tired as adults do because they totally connect with their energy in their play without all the analysing.

When we are in our bodies and not our minds, we can fully engage and enjoy the moment, simply energy without our own labels added on, this is why holidays are so critical. It's worth re-reading this to fully grasp the implication of how our energy unfolds within us. This is how when people get absorbed with mental activities and have less fun in their lives, how this separation and disconnection unfolds. The more it controls our lives the more we lose our connection with our 'inner child' and with the light-hearted part of ourselves, this is an important concept to ponder over.

How the Benefits of Self-Pleasuring Outweigh Masturbation

Males have been accustomed to ejaculating for release and have been told genital release is a "medical" necessity. Considering this, the habit of masturbation may be difficult to change to self-pleasuring when they are accustomed to a quick "wank" to release tension normally. However, the evidence is overwhelming that males develop physical problems related to stress, which affects their lives because they disconnect with their energy. Frequent masturbation disconnects males from themselves just as smoking does, as it is something they do that involves only one part of them and not the whole of their energy. This is disconnection.

A common old wives' tale says that masturbating often leads to blindness, which of course is false. However, there is a small pocket of truth in this. During masturbation, energy accumulates, and the focus is on releasing it. However, a male doesn't procreate every time he ejaculates they have a built-in program for procreation connected with ejaculation. This default male program means a male thinks the more he "cums," the more of a stud it makes him but instead he is disconnecting his energy wasting and feeling drained that males feel soon after sex. The truth, however, is that he can still have all the pleasure simply by getting his energy to Row through all his body by using 'the orgasmic effect' method that gives full-body orgasm instead of the usual genital climax.

Consider when you were in your twenties. Your energy was rampant, and you were hopefully excited about life then, so whenever you met a special someone and were intimate, the feeling was not only alive in your genitals but also through your whole body. You probably didn't really notice when that feeling started subsiding over a few years and became localized mainly in your genital area. By the time you were in your thirties, the disconnection slowly began to be noticeable as the general internal excitement in the rest of your body subsided.

Disconnection creeps up slowly, unnoticeably, and when sexual fantasy overtakes feelings of connection, the feelings get lost and can sometimes turn into sexual addiction or just the urge for sexual release from ongoing tension. Hence the urge for seeking sexual release as preference and frequently visiting adult services.

Men in their forties develop a very different need. They begin to realize they are not lasting as long as they'd like and worry their relationships are suffering due to their underperformance. They will often seek alternatives to correct this. This can often start happening as early as the early thirties. As males get older, they discover that sex is not as frequently available to them as it was when they were in their twenties or early thirties. They have to pay for it, or they don't have the time due to work and family commitments. While the stress continues to build, the opportunity to release and counteract the stress is reduced.

For example, each time a male looks at a sexy girl at a club, at the beach, or on TV, his genitals are active without his really paying attention because he is used to his genitals always stirring as a sign of energy. Everything we do is energy; even a simple tapping of fingers involves energy. Try tapping your finger for a while and then stop to see how the energy builds up when you stop.

Simple energy management can shift these ongoing problems, as any acupuncturist trained to deal with energy blockages will tell you. Self-pleasuring is not only the total opposite of masturbation, but engaging in it several times a day brings you relief in addition to increasing your energy levels and relaxing you, benefiting every area of your body. Practicing the self-pleasuring technique teaches your cells to spread the energy through your body, refreshing, recharging, and energizing it in the process. Using this method "installs" within your cells the memory of a new program of how to spread your vital energy rather than draining it away. It's an easy five-minutes-a-day benefit for your system that makes you feel balanced, harmonized, and refreshed, just as a good night's sleep does.

This video will give you staying power with this energy method; it demonstrates the techniques and also includes an e-book: http://theorgasmiceffect.com.

Additionally when males are stressed, they do not pay any attention to their diets or their eating habits, so their health suffers as a result of bad eating habits, that seem to go hand in hand with work related stresses. This topic will be expanded upon in the last chapter.

The Self-Pleasuring Pathway to Energy

The ancient art of self-pleasuring is about moving the energy up through the body, and it is better understood when looking at the chakra system. Masturbation can be compared to a linear movement during which the energy accumulates and exits, and its only pathway is the base and sacral centre chakras.

This is why when energy is not used in sex it does build up leading to tension in the body, *creating shorter staying power due to tension at the time of ejaculation.* This is because the body is automatically programmed and the energy follows a default pathway and automatically exits when sexual energy is released during sex.

Self-pleasuring, on the other hand, is the moving of energy throughout the body. As this energy moves through the body, it moves upward and spreads through all the cells, continuing to connect through the chakras. Many have described the experience of this energy moving; as bliss. When practiced with regularity, self-pleasuring not only energizes the body but also raises its energy to a new level. Energy moving through the chakras can be physically observed on the person's face and they describe it as "a light, Roaty, relaxed" feeling or "light, tingly peace."

Learning anything new requires practice, and only with practice can this method become the new default program in your body. This is when bliss is frequently experienced—and just a few minutes of daily practice moving this energy is all it takes. It gives the male prolonged ability, enabling him to increase his staying power from two minutes to twenty minutes with a few weeks' practice. This experience of bliss is a practice that gives a male a nice feeling of connection to himself and his partner, and the best part is that the male has learnt the ejaculation control all men seek.

Self Pleasuring Origins from Ancient Times

The self-pleasuring method described under the heading of "Benefits of Connecting and Maintaining Energy" describes how practising this method slowly disperses energy. The person feels lighter, more energized, and happier. Because the energy is Rowing, tiredness is reduced and aging slows because the energy is moving, Rowing, and spreading in the body. It's all common sense, and you will find this information well documented in the ancient Tantra texts, not from modern practitioners. Many health- aware people and health practitioners know about this but don't practice it because it is an art that requires persistent personal discipline.

I had a boyfriend many years ago who practiced the self-pleasuring method naturally, and I used to ask him why he didn't ejaculate. His answer was that the pleasure and enjoyment was doubly increased and continued to increase when he focused on moving his energy through his body and avoided ejaculation. I later looked up "Tantra" and discovered that:

> *In ancient times, sultans who had large harems would put a master in charge of the eunuchs to a test. The master had to drink wine through his penis and hold it before releasing it through his penis, thus demonstrating his masterful control and disciplined power.*

This ability demonstrated the control he had over himself and consequently over other areas of his life, as this is not a feat that can be mastered in a few months. I have translated 'this feat' into the simple techniques you can learn at the site : theorgasmiceffect.com based on a simple principle that energizes and relaxes your body at the same time when you practise it daily, this is where your good feelings come from and give you all the additional benefits.

I've had several clients who had developed prostate problems, and when they began practicing the 'orgasmic effect techniques', their tests showed their symptoms had significantly reduced. One client said his doctor told him he didn't have a prostate problem—the previous tests "must have been wrong."

Overcoming Mental Distractions during Sex

As our thinking process consists mainly of images we will associate an image to an experience, this is how funny comments and jokes, in offices and classrooms, gain attention where boys use sexual innuendos, causing their minds to create an image they laugh about. However, when we don't have an image of an experience, the mind will automatically manufacture one so the joke can become even funnier.

As previously mentioned we generally don't think in the middle of sex, as we are enjoying in our bodies, not in our minds. This is because when we are in our body there is nothing for our mind to analyse, judge, assess, or criticize (hopefully). That is how we can know we are not in our mind at the time!

When judgement, criticism, analysis, or assessment is going on, this is a signal that your mind is in full swing. If the time is not appropriate to stop this process, simply put your attention on what you are doing, it will change everything. The only way to achieve this is by enjoying what you are feeling and learning to engage the mind with the body. This is when the *ahhhh* feeling comes in, and verbalizing it gets the sensation of it into your body and stops your mind from engaging in the judgement game.

Think of when you say *ahhhh* during a shower, when that nice warm water instantly relaxes you. People also say it when putting on fresh clothes or getting into a warm bed or simply sitting down to a coffee or a piece of cake. See if you can be more present to your *ahhhh* feeling; this will bring you more in touch with your enjoyment energy and use the feel-good feeling more frequently.

This is actually the 'being state' I was discussing previously and is the surest way of keeping your health and vitality at optimal levels when you engage with this part of yourself i.e. taking a breath and allowing yourself to enjoy 'a moment in time'. Remind yourself that this enhanced orgasmic feeling is your energized self, your health, abundance, and longevity rolled into one, and it can be used on a daily basis, to energize you, not just occasionally!

To Conclude: Masturbation expels energy, and men feel drained as a result. With the self-pleasuring method on the other hand, energy spreads through the body. As this energy moves and spreads, it gives men a more connected feeling of satisfaction as it continues to connect through the chakras. When practiced with regularity, self-pleasuring energizes the body and raises the energy level that balances the body, giving greater health and well-being. This is the orgasmic effect technique.

Ways to Reconnect and Gain Strength

Family or any other kind of outing is when connection begins. Think of the movies that touch us, father-and-son activities, listening to elders' lessons of life, going for long nature walks, swimming, even exercising outdoors; they all begin to bring connection back to us. This is a good beginning but not the solution.

Taking up an activity with all your heart will slowly put you in touch with your wonder and delight, an expanding and reconnecting type of energy present within each of us! This opens up gratitude and appreciation. It's from here that love unfolds. Love is a gentle relaxation from the inside, and it happens in the region of the heart. When we do something from the heart, it tends to open us into kindness and softness. This is a big turn-on for women, and as a result of this energetic feeling inside, we tend to become more open and able to open to fun, joy, and light-heartedness, a word that explains it all. A lightness of heart means a release of the burdens that cause depression, illness, and worry and lead to aches, pains, and unhappiness. We don't need a doctor to tell us this, nor do we need drugs to open our hearts.

Essential Methods for Reconnecting

Whatever activity you do to maintain connectedness must be something you do regularly and enjoy. Activities including tai chi and qigong promote this inner connection. These slow exercises cause you to connect with a deeper part of yourself, and you slowly begin to understand what connection really feels like. Mothers with young children experience the closest connection and feel it inside. When you engage in charity work, you experience the same feelings. A holiday that allows you to step into nature and breathe fresh air can relax you for at least a week. You can do this with regular walks or yoga classes. We generally don't associate people who do yoga with having any serious health issues such as heart problems, do we?

When families grow up, that connected feeling can continue through grandchildren. However, if parents start to live through their children, they are not connecting with themselves directly. Children leaving home to lead their lives can be a major source of grievance for parents. Parents who have been living their lives through their children haven't taken the time to get to know themselves, and they often don't know how to fill that gap later in their lives and consequently become very lonely.

Loneliness is withdrawal from life. You want to ensure against this illness, which leads to physical problems. This is the main reason for engaging in a hobby or having something you look forward to, like giving your time to a charity. Living from your heart makes you feel you are part of something bigger than yourself. When you contribute time to a good cause, you involve a higher part of you and get in touch with your inner being or spirit, the real you, the joyous and free part of you that comes into play and gets you to feel connected with yourself.

People who stay in unfulfilling jobs find their energy becoming stagnant, which results in disinterest and lethargy. Unless there is something outside work that will pick up their energy, such as an engaging sport, dancing, or some other interest or activity they are passionate about, their unchecked low energy leads to lack of interest, which is the beginning of depression, lack of self-respect, and loneliness.

I knew an elderly lady in her early 70ys, a sweet soul whose only occupation was getting dressed up to go for walks and shopping. She was always on the lookout for expensive shoes or handbags though her residence was very meagre. Whenever she was asked if she would like to visit her home country, go on a trip, or take a holiday with a group, she would always disdainfully respond that she was not the least bit interested. There was no society she wanted to be part of or any interest she'd take up that involved people. One day she fell over, and after that, she was afraid to go outside. She nursed her fear to the point that it prevented her from living. Fainting fits and hospital trips started to replace her walks, and it seemed her hospital trips somehow got her to connect with people. There was really nothing wrong with her health; it was her way of thinking that prevented her from taking an interest in activities and slowly brought about her demise. The deterioration of her health stemmed from her disinterest in making an effort to do something more than just walking to shops and back. This is an example of disconnection.

The Self-Pleasuring Method Exercise

To begin, allow yourself to go into the usual relaxed feeling mode, you can do this sitting or standing up. Your object should be to keep the energy moving, so you are not masturbating with the intention of ejaculating. You do this simply by rubbing the genitals. Stop as soon as you feel the energy building up. Place your other hand on your heart and breathe the energy in by taking a deep breath. Repeat this several times until you begin to get the feeling of your energy moving slowly up your body. You are not going to feel this immediately; this is not instant coffee, so you need to give it time and practice. You don't expect to learn carpentry or painting in one sitting; everything takes practice to accomplish to some degree of satisfaction. It's important not to rush your effort to get results.

You will see how the nice feelings slowly become automatic by simply touching your genitals and your heart at the same time. This allows you to consciously connect to a nice feeling. To enhance this feeling, bring your mind to something you really love to do, like a special walk or a nice holiday you had or are about to have. Focus on anything that gives you a good feeling. This could be an outing with friends, or a party—anything of a fun nature. Connect to this feeling each time you place your hand on your heart during this exercise.

Do this exercise several times in one go. It will take you a few minutes at any one time to get that refreshing feeling on the inside, and you may repeat it during your day as it gives your energy a natural lift. Don't we have coffee breaks to break away from ongoing routine tasks be they work or family related? You can do this in that way.

This simple method also enhances your creativity, enthusiasm, and drive. It energizes your organs and gives you a greater sense of vitality. It brings your whole energy into greater focus, enabling you to be more present in everything you do. That is why it makes the sexual experience better than ever.

This begins a new way of experiencing lovemaking, and it takes your energy to a new level. Practicing this method will enable you to feel more deeply and experience a heart connection and loving relationships. This simple method teaches you to hook up to your joy at will and connects you with pleasurable emotions. It's like playing more than one note on a scale, which is what enhances your sexual experience.

This simple practice is a life-balancing system; it gives the body a recharge, promotes deep inner healing, and revives sexual pleasure, inner warmth, and connection with your partner by connecting to your love energy by moving your energy to the heart chakra.

Using Your Orgasmic Energy in Daily Life

You are basically learning how to master this, and your partner can learn it also. It's a lot easier for women to learn this method, because women do the full-body orgasm relatively naturally where energy travels through their bodies. Generally, female energy is not half as blocked as male energy. When males practice the orgasmic effect, their energy slowly disperses even if blockage has already begun.

There are several ways to activate your "internal rejuvenator." These steps will charge your body and with daily practice help increase your longevity. Longevity is keeping the heart active with unobstructed vital energy. The steps involved in maintaining this balance keep your energy vibrating at a higher level, which means the food you eat is not the primary factor. As discussed above, many activities raise our energy, but we need the higher levels that involve feeling to make our hearts healthy and balanced.

Here are the 'feeling levels' to additionally include with your daily exercise plus your positive social routines and work ethic.

1. Be conscious of appreciation and grateful for the small things in your life, thus connecting with life.
2. Find things you can enjoy wholeheartedly.
3. Get involved in something that involves and helps others so you are adding benefit outside yourself.

4. Have a loving partner or good friend that you can do little things for him/her, stimulating this joy energy factor.

5. Be appreciative and express appreciation to people. This opens the door to joyful energy by connecting you to your heart.

Activating Orgasms for Women

This is a good practice to have on hand, as it comes in very useful during those times when you might want to rekindle a relationship or you are getting ready for a hot evening and are feeling a little apprehensive or tense.

Begin by massaging your nipples. Try not to indulge in sexual fantasy unless you are looking forward to a hot evening, but simply enjoy the sensation. Keep in mind the reason behind what you are doing here and stay with the nice feeling cascading through your body. You can do this under a shower for a bit, or upon waking in the morning, or just standing by the window facing the sun, breathing fresh air before having a shower, or starting your day the way you usually do.

Try holding onto this nice feeling of good energy by then taking this into your day. When you succeed, you will indeed feel very different from when you started. Practice this daily, and you will find you can turn the method into a mood enhancer. The more you practice, the more you will find that you have successfully mastered this nice pleasurable technique, which can eventually become automatic.

The Real Inner and Outer You

Your heart is the real you, the being part of you, which is opposite to the doing part or the 'doing state' which happens in your head. As I have mentioned previously, we never say, "I'm doing in love" its something we feel not do. We say, "I'm being in love," "I'm being with a friend," "I'm being on a holiday," so we are feeling this rather than doing it, enjoyment is the feeling, it's how we feel when we are in love or holiday of with a friend. Another way to understand the being part is to say; we are a human being not a human doing. The doing part is the head part: it's what we do, where we live, our homes, our families, our bodies, our nationalities, all that belongs to the world, and we have no control over that. We may think so, but in reality, we have very little control.

The heart or feeling part is all we have that belongs to us. This being part of us is what we come into the world with and its the only part that we take with us. We experience feelings with the being part of us; that's why people pay a lot of money for expensive holidays, cars, or apartments. It's just to get that great feeling, at the end of it, be that from a great trip or a holiday or winning money.

If you want to activate or be able to switch that feeling on you can, by practicing activating your orgasmic energy daily. Just as you shower daily to feel refreshed or you use the toilet daily to stay regular, it's the same with this. If you want to stay in control of your inner good feelings, this simple exercise is what enables you to raise your energy to get to that state within you. When you do this regularly, you will love how your newfound practice gives you that nice, balanced, zing feeling you'll never want to be without. It completely changes your life. You will begin to see life from the perspective of who you really are, which does away with anxiety, confusion, anger, and depression. All it requires is getting up in the morning, walking to an open window, and breathing the freshness into your lungs and doing the ten minutes of connection with activating your orgasmic energizing or alternatively doing meditation.

Take additional conscious breaths during the day, recall the nice *feeling* on the inside, and think of something you love to do—a situation, a walk, a holiday, or someone you have fond feelings for. This helps you stay connected to lovingness, your life force and inner being naturally and easily.

It is therefore vital that you have something you do for relaxation that is pleasurable and rejuvenating for the body and involves your heart. Yoga is about the best medicine because it connects you to the inner part of you and doesn't involve outer thinking, as do most exercises that require increasing muscle mass, speed, or stamina. Just as during sleep, the mind is not engaging but relaxing, so during yoga the body gets a chance to rebalance from whatever stress or situation you face.

When these emotions come up during yoga, you have time to exhale the pent-up emotion or stress that may arise when focusing on the breath. This is the main reason it's the easiest of exercises for rebalancing and reconnecting rather than strenuous exercises that require more energy but do not give you even half the benefits yoga will. Yoga allows you to rebalance the inner you far more easily.

To Conclude: You can charge up your body daily with longevity by using your 'internal rejuvenator' with the simple exercises and achieve this by practicing moving your energy to your heart daily. These are easy steps to achieving connectedness, which is part of the internal energy of gratitude and aliveness. Yoga is one of the simplest means to maintain all of the above. Engaging in heart-warming hobbies on a regular basis also activates the alive-feeling and additionally gives you something to look forward to as part of your life.

Chapter 4

Balance for Life in Sex and Relationships

Love is a cohesive force that acts as a rejuvenator for our whole system. It helps us maintain stronger health, gives longevity and greater joy, and creates a sense of relaxation, adventure, and spontaneity in our daily lives.

Experiencing true freedom in relationships and our lives is our heritage! But do we want this freedom? For us to have freedom, we need to make changes to fit in with a new way of being. Any change needs a framework to work within to help us achieve amazing quality of life on all levels. Our bodies were designed perfect we need to recognize this internally, and can activate our subconscious minds to stay in touch with this truth daily, in order to be certain of this fact.

What you have read so far has given you ways and means to get in touch with this truth. Otherwise, you can believe TV ads that say illness 'happens', and when it happens, just take this or that pill and it will be fixed, or continue to take more pills, never mind the side effects or whether the pills work.

However, every uncomfortable thing that occurs inside us is a result of what we have ignored, overlooked, or denied. This is when we do not wish to see and understand the deeper meanings behind what is occurring in family or work situations, for example.

As I have stated in several ways already to have success in any area of life, you must identify and remove the saboteurs or blockages that stand in the way of your success. This also applies to health; you can have greater control over your life just by putting the decision into your subconscious and reminding yourself of this fact automatically. Setting up a program for physical health and longevity is key to making changes for creating balance in your personal relationships and your life on all levels.

We do not make these choices overnight; we do so only when we have noticed how the same things repeat over and over until they become uncomfortable. When we decide that this is no one else's fault, and can take responsibility and recognize that we can correct the situation over a period of time, then as long as we are improving we are stepping forward. This may mean participating in personal development workshops. Such steps change the way we perceive our goals and affect our vision for prosperity, which leads us to undergoing a big shift for the better. Are you prepared to do whatever it takes? Are you ready for the best journey of your life?

Developing spiritual needs creates balance and increases inner strength, and by simply using meditation twice a week, positive changes begin to appear. Meditation can be as simple as sitting and listening to your breathing for about five to eight minutes to begin with. Focusing on your breathing is all it takes initially. This slows the mind and relaxes the body, and you will find it to be an effective way of resolving daily issues especially when you do this in the early morning.

It's better to work with a mentor, especially a trainer who can incorporate all this into your busy life schedule and guide you on mental, emotional, and physical levels.

Exercise of some form is a wonderful secondary means of maintaining positive energy. We need balance even with exercise. This is why I refer to yoga a lot, as it's the most direct way to create balance in mind and body, and a way of creating harmony in emotions and health as well.

Life works when we are balanced with ourselves, when we are in disharmony out of kilter with life we affect the ones we love around us.

What a Woman Wants from a Man

It's not just intercourse a woman wants from her man. Anyone can do that. A woman wants to experience feelings of ecstasy that will transcend her thoughts of time and space. She wants her man to touch her heart and know her deepest desires. Every man wants to provide this for his woman, but most do not know how to give her an uplifting experience in which both reach elevated states beyond the sexual. Once a man achieves this, the relationship reaches new heights of love and ecstasy, which not only gives him the upper hand over all other men but allows him to access higher states of pleasure for himself as well.

Sexual pleasure these days is more than just physical contact; combining his pleasure and enabling his partner to reach orgasmic heights is more of a turn-on for him than just pleasing himself. Feeling love within the heart is opening the heart to the doorway of greater power.

It's not about learning a variety of positions. Sexual power lies in allowing the heart to open, and we can achieve this by steadily experiencing deeper levels of pleasure, enabling partners to go to deeper levels of intimacy. We can achieve this by being more open and honest with one another with inne feelings, bearing in mind that feelings are energy based.

When Heart Connection Is Not There

We cannot experience ecstasy when the heart connection is not there. New relationships are magical because of their possibilities. The heart is free for a short while; then it slowly closes as mind takes over with analysing, judging, processing, criticizing, and assessing. The relationship gradually goes stale as a result.

Connecting with his heart gives a man a simple means of reconnecting to his internal energy, which is what turns women on. And it's what additionally gives him the benefit of lasting power in the bedroom. These powerful tools help males regain lost connection with themselves (their inner being). Reconnecting with a new relationship can be difficult for anyone stuck in past memories and out of balance with a broken or a wounded heart. This is a wonderful and new method for re-awakening your energy, which gradually heals and allows you to reconnect naturally and easily with yourself before you try with another.

People search to find a connection with a soul mate and feel many potential partners are missing that vital link, so I have included this anonymous quote from a calendar that describes connection:

> *"It's the deeper levels I'm interested in, and I could see you were not able to look into my eyes on a soul level. It was easier to say nothing rather than find a way to explain it to you…"*

Hence, we first need to resolve issues and free blockages, without which we can glimpse only a hint of what's possible within ourselves before we can see it within the other person.

Healing Touch: Another Aspect of Sexual Energy—Exercise

Spreading your sexual energy through your body can be a shortcut to an energy boost you may need, for example, before an interview or meeting. This is a quick-access exercise below.

- Start by feeling the warmth of the hands together, then move that warmth along and spread it around the body.

Begin by placing your hands on your belly, feeling the warmth, and then increasing their warmth until you can put your hands on any part of your body and create a warm, healing feeling.

- See yourself as light energy connected to the sun, as though you were standing in a beam of light, feeling connected to it. Open and close your eyes as though you were bringing this feeling into your being, around you as well as within you.

- Feel how you'd like to connect to a loving feeling inside you, and just simply stroke yourself at the same time by putting your arms around yourself as though you were hugging yourself. It works—try it! You can begin to feel the lovely, warm, fuzzy feeling creeping in.

- Notice how feelings are associated with touch. To illustrate how we forget to use this touch on ourselves, do this little touch exercise frequently: touch your arm, stroke your hand against your belly or heart, saying to yourself "I am a loving, caring, gentle person, and I deserve a wonderful, caring relationship."

At this point, you may be associating the way you may have been touched in your childhood. If tears come up, let yourself simply heal by continuing the touch, gently stoking whatever emotional pain is associated with that part of your body. The more frequently you do this, even if you're sitting with some inner discomfort, the more the internal healing will take place, and you will never need to visit a doctor. You are effectively releasing stagnant energy that would otherwise have created some energy stuckness, eventually affecting your health. This is why it's important to do this exercise with some regularity.

The *Healing of the Inner Child* CD takes you through an internal healing process and allows you to release the built-up energy relating to early child experiences you might be unknowingly carrying. Listening to the CD each time a memory comes up will lighten internal burdens, and your breathing will feel a lot lighter until you feel one day something suddenly lets go internally. See: http://www.essentiallifeskills.com/online_shop.html.

Hooking Up to Your Joy Energy

Hooking up to your joy energy at will means using emotions to open yourself to more pleasurable all- over sensations. It's like playing more than one note on a scale, and it enhances your sexual experience.

As I've mentioned before gratitude and appreciation are higher notes on the emotional scale. We forget to be grateful for many things in our lives and instead focus on negative images. Instead we could be engaging and enjoying the company of a special friend, or expressing genuine feelings to our partners, which actually increases sexual tension and connectedness. This is what brings 'these notes on the scale' into greater harmony with the sexual dynamic we felt long ago, and it is key to this healing-touch exercise. Expressing and sincerely communicating through our eyes while expressing our feelings is the magic that increases the sexual level between our partners and us.

Making eye contact with anyone you are communicating with is not just a sign of respect but adds more openness and warmer communication and lets the other person trust you and feel more comfortable as well as having better relations. Connecting to your love energy consciously gives your body a recharge, promotes deep inner healing, and revives sexual pleasure, warmth, and connection with your partner. Hence, when you act wholeheartedly, it brings your life energy into greater focus, and makes the sexual experience better than ever. *Think of it as intimacy; "into me see."*

This way it becomes a beginning to a new way of experiencing lovemaking and takes your energy to a new level, with sex being only part of lovemaking instead of using sex just for comfort or releasing tension.

Tips for Igniting Passion in Your Relationship

Men; has sex become, a tired, old routine? If you're floundering in the bedroom and want to make bedtime count, you need to learn a few skills. Sex is part of the way you express yourself, and you want to be comfortable with how you do so. You want your partner to respond favourably to your sexual interest; women love to be entertained and aroused and usually rely on men to make things interesting. Taking control of the situation and showing her how you can make her sizzle will demonstrate you are the guy who can give her the best time in the world. Ignite her passion and yours at the same time. It's not as hard as you think, and it's a lot of fun. All it takes is preparation and a desire to make things work.

Have you noticed how you can feel almost invincible when a surge of passion runs through you? When your energy is focused on something or someone, you get very excited, or the opposite when you feel powerless and your energy sinks and you draw away. Passion can ignite you on the spur of the moment, its quite a powerful feeling and when passion fills you, it can be quite overwhelming, as though the energy is cascading through you, providing an invigorating rush that lasts for some time.

Sexual passion is a heightened sense of desire fuelled by raw personal energy; it is the powerful driving force behind our intent and actions. We think our partners or lovers cause these energy surges, but in fact, we cause these feelings. We are not normally aware that we can activate the feeling of passion by ourselves, at will; instead, we generally accept that someone or something else is in control of our passions. Isn't that what happens when we attend parties? We look forward to them because they make us feel good and give us a rush. Preparing for a passionate evening is not unlike preparing a fine meal, or a party. We prepare the ingredients and follow the recipe. We take care to plan everything carefully, set the mood, and go through the motions.

The environment you prepare for your partner/lover will have a big effect on her, and you want her in a relaxed mood so you will have a great night. Setting up your special night with a partner is all about creating a special ambiance of music, food, conversation, a pleasant or surprising location, and of course yourself. Treat your day or evening with your partner by getting in the mood.

Just as a party unfolds slowly, you too need to avoid rushing your special night. Patience is everything. Women see patient men as being strong and in control of themselves. By rushing or pushing things too fast, you give the impression you are inconsiderate and unsure of yourself. Be aware of the signals your partner is giving you. Don't rush in and spoil what might slowly develop on its own.

Trust your senses. When the day or evening is progressing smoothly and effortlessly, good feelings will give you a clear indication you are succeeding with your plan. Just as your 'party feelings' begin to surface, you will begin to feel relaxed and feel your defences drop, and you will relax more.

Sexual passion is the same. If you are comfortable with yourself, you will find that your partner will be comfortable with you too. Always be sure your partner is comfortable with how far you go. By being aware of your partner's signals, you will avoid taking the wrong turn and spending the rest of the evening alone, wondering where you went wrong.

Sexual Mastery Comes with Practice

Sexual mastery can be learnt. By practicing these skills, you will over time get better and better. To start, learn the effect your words and actions have on your partner/lover. You need to learn how to read your partner's signals accurately; it is the difference between success and failure.

Don't be afraid to ask your partner how s/he's feeling or if she's enjoying whatever you are "serving up" for your eventful evening. S/he will see you as very considerate, and this will open deeper levels of communication between you. You might feel uncomfortable asking questions such as "Am I doing it right?" during sexual interaction. However, if you don't ask, you will never progress beyond what you know. Therefore, ask if you want to learn, grow, and improve yourself. Be aware that acts of intimacy are not just about your pleasure; they are also about learning if your lover is having as good a time as you are.

Compare the situation to having a massage. You would most likely prefer to pay for a massage than have someone massage you with no sensitivity or care. When masseuses are not sensitive, their massages can feel quite coarse and give the impression they have no idea what they're doing. You can also sense if the other person is not present, not in the moment, with you.

Be present with all you involve yourself in, and you will see the big difference this makes to your love life and sexual mastery. By talking idly about irrelevant things or doing something distracting like switching on the TV, you may be changing the mood, and when you do this, it will change the atmosphere to one that feels rather flat for her, and it may leave you wondering what happened to all the build-up.

The More Thought Energy You Put In, the Quicker and Greater the Rewards

You will enjoy yourself more when you put all your energy into whatever you are doing, and you will feel the difference the next day. You will find you are more satisfied with yourself. This also applies to things outside the bedroom you put all yourself into.

Sex is fun, as is romance, so make every encounter with your lover a fun and exciting activity. Think about what you are trying to achieve. If you want only some quick fun, recognize you may not see this person again. If you want to see that person again, take time to plan. Preparation is what sets the mood. Hoping it will just work is like hoping you will get good results at school. Preparation will gear you up for a mind-blowing and memorable experience with the person you love and desire.

Good Advice : If you seem to miss out and not get the results you wish, ask a trusted, older, female friend. Women love to give advice about romance. Just make sure not to ask a woman who is just getting out of a relationship that went sour or you may get a post-mortem on her relationship.

To Conclude: Sexual mastery requires practicing the learnt skills with your partner. You need to learn how to read your partner's signals accurately, which is the difference between success and failure. Take your time and listen to one another especially when a disquieting memory comes up; this is a very healing way to lighten an internal burden. Bringing it up at 'an appropriate time' promotes inner healing and a stronger connection with your partner

Tips for Guys about Prolonging

Enjoying what you are doing *with all your heart* is the key to *prolonging orgasm*. It's the key because your heart is the power source, and moving energy from your genitals or base chakra to your heart chakra is what gives the body ongoing connection to your power source. Don't try reasoning with this, as it will interfere with the joy energy, the "inner child" energy.

If guys only knew how turned on women are by men who connect with their hearts during intimacy! Men generally agree they are disconnected from their emotions during sex, as though their genitals were somehow separate from the rest of them.

When you express appreciation to someone or they express it to you, you open that magic door to your heart, the joy energy, which stimulates the body. It also promotes healing and enthusiasm, gives you longevity, and is the magic link to lasting power in the bedroom.

You can help yourself by engaging in activities such as; weightlifting, aerobics, Pilates, tai chi, dancing— whatever you fancy—as long as you do it on a regular basis. "I used to do…" is what I hear from males who have stopped regular exercise. Choose any physical activity that keeps your energy vital and that you can do regularly. The options of light exercise with groups and sports are endless!

Clowning around allows light-heartedness, and there is a legitimate time to do that. You can let yourself fun around like a child, so give yourself permission to do so, and if your partner is present make sure you are involving her and not just thinking you are. You must make time to do this so you are not hurrying some other activity that will cut off your play. When I dance, I rejoice on the dance floor, fully connecting to the child energy. It's good for the soul to allow yourself to laugh and be silly as a child frequently.

Six Ways to Make Your Body More Desirable to a Woman

If you want your partner to do all the erotic pleasurable things you constantly fantasise about, here are a few tips.

1. Washing will make you smell a lot nicer to your partner during sex, and she will enjoy your company much more. Always take a shower early on.

2. Some couples enjoy showering together as part of foreplay. Have towels ready for additional spillage in case she prefers the bath.

3. A hairy body does not mean you need to shave all your hair; some females like it.

4. Floss your teeth and use mouthwash, especially if you are a smoker. Most girls don't like kissing an ashtray. Use aftershave.

5. If you are hairy, around your genitals consider shaving some of the "undergrowth" as trimmed pubic hair shows you are looking after yourself.

6. If you shave your back or chest, as some men do, your hair will re-grow in time and will come in prickly, which is very uncomfortable for your special lady. Ask her before you do this.

If your foreskin is very sensitive after ejaculation, visit a doctor; there are easy ways to remedy this situation. A large percentage of males are not aware of accumulated genital odour, as I have discussed earlier. If you get into these good habits, your girl will never be put off by what may be overlooked in the heat of the moment, (especially with oral sex, which can happen spontaneously).

Some men's backs and chests are covered with hair. Some women love hairy guys and can feel very safe and secure with their cavemen. Each man has a potential mate out there and needs to know the right woman will love him for the way he is—on the exterior as well as the interior.

Ideas for Creating Sizzling More-Pleasurable Experiences

If your partner is going to give you an erotic massage, don't have a heavy meal right before. Have a snack and save the meal for later, perhaps after a bath, so you can both relax and set the mood for the next phase. Here are a few tips for setting the mood.

- Don't overeat. Having a heavy meal before sex will make you drowsy. The mood can drop or totally disappear without you even realizing it.
- See if she'd like you to buy her a sexy bra and panties, then encourage her to put them on so she can see the appreciation on your face. She will continue wanting to display her sexiness to you and avoid flirtation elsewhere.
- Massage is a great way to get her to relax and for both of you to enjoy gentle foreplay to enhance the mood. Improve your massaging skills, and encourage her to massage you as well.
- Aromatic candles work well with a bath. Have many clean towels handy; you'll need them.
- Make a habit of buying a bottle of something you both enjoy, but keep in mind that alcohol is a mood enhancer, not the focus.
- Be inventive and creative. Ladies love novelty and the unexpected, so have chocolates on hand and a silk scarf for an added touch at the right moment.
- Have the feel-alive feeling always present; focus on staying relaxed but switched on, meaning avoid hallucinogenics. They may seem fun at the time, but when they wear off, so does the reality of the moment. If you want that special

moment to last, be real rather than spaced out; it will have the opposite effect in the long term.

- Do out-of-body experiences by yourself, not with your partner; this will distance you from one another. Trust me on this!
- Passion can stagnate if you go too slow and vanish if you go too fast. Timing is everything, so learn from your own timing and keep adjusting it.
- Consider using sex toys; they can be great mood setters and fun.

What Turns Your Partner On?

Here are a few roles younger women tend to play. These are trends that girls especially, can fall into and some younger gay males, and take themselves seriously when acting out. If you can playfully identify this role by playing up to her, it may help her realize she is living a fantasy. You can have some fun with this role-playing until she is ready to correct herself. Some girls have been indulged by their parents and are not consciously aware they are using this type of behaviour until it is exposed in a harmless game.

- **The Princess**: She likes you to treat her like a princess, meaning you can never do enough for her.
- **The Cinderella**: She wants to be rescued by her Prince Charming and could become dependent even for simple things.
- **The Goddess**: She wants you to worship her and will behave as if she's unreachable and aloof.
- **The Drama Queen**: This applies to both sexes. He or she likes to perform to get attention at any time. Always a bit of a handful.

- **The Cougar**: A title generally applied to older women, usually from their mid-forties to late fifties, ladies on the look out / on the prowl for younger men.

Spend some time working out what "type" your lady/guy is; it pays off. Decide how best to treat him/her rather than cater to negative connotations. Whether you are going to indulge all her whims or simply on special occasions, you should draw her attention to how her behaviour affects your day and your relationship with her. This may be a lot of fun, and you can certainly use it to gain each other's favour and please one another.

She Wants You to Express Your Passion

Women like attention from their man, and they love genuine attention. Passion communicates to a women that their man is not only interested in them but also enjoy their company and want to be close to them.

Women pay attention when their men express their feelings. It's not what they buy that counts; it's the attention they show their women and the way they express their maleness and consideration. You can do this in the small things you do, for example, noticing what she likes and doesn't like. When you share with her what you are sensitive and passionate about, she will naturally become more interested in and sensitive to you. The less you express and share with her, the less loved and appreciated she will feel. It's no good saying, "But I don't know what to say." You don't have to think about what to say to your close friends just relax and be yourself; that's who you are, and being who you are will allow her to relax and be herself with you.

Why Women Are Moody

Women love to experience the totality of their emotions on all levels. Dogs' bark, clouds rain, and women get moody. Get used to it. If your woman is in a strange or bad mood, ask her to talk about it and don't take no for an answer. You are emotionally involved with her, so learn to talk about stuff. Put your cards on the table and encourage her to do the same.

Trying to hide your bad habits will be a wedge in your relationship. Everyone eventually detects when something is not sitting right, although someone might not be able to articulate it right away. When these gaps appear because of things unsaid, relationships begin to go astray, so be open and try to discuss whatever you have been avoiding. A good policy is to be clear with your intentions so you are not carrying an unspoken agenda into the next day. You will be surprised how supportive your woman can be when you open with "I meant to tell you yesterday that the reason I said what I said was …" *She will love you for it.*

Women love shopping—this is a given—so take her shopping and simply observe her rather than think about how much she is spending or how bored you are going to be. The best time to shop with her is when you want to give her a treat. She will adore you for the attention you give her by just being there with her. If you indulge her fancy and go shopping with her, let her know what the limit of your patience is. Set some boundaries and review this after an hour or so, or this will drive you nuts. Setting boundaries makes things easier in the long run, and she will see you as being supportive and involved rather than dispassionate or disinterested.

These tips will help you become the lover and partner you want to be. You'll make some mistakes along the way, but don't be too hard on yourself when something doesn't go the way you planned. Learn from your mistakes and refine your approach.

To Conclude: By taking care of the little details and preparing for your special, pleasurable times, you will double your pleasure and satisfaction. The little details become good habits, and a few years down the track, these tips on planning your night will continue to serve you well.

Guide to Prolonging Orgasm for Women: The Power of Love

To achieve prolonged orgasm, a woman needs emotional connection with her partner long before sexual intimacy commences. She needs sexual foreplay to become stimulated on an emotional level first; this builds an intimate connection for her. Most women are motivated through their hearts, and the openness they feel in sexual experiences is due to their heart and mind connections.

As women's sexual fantasies rely on emotional, dream-type fantasies, they will sense a deeper connection to their men on how they feel these fantasies through their bodies. Every woman fantasises, and some will see the marriage and children scenario from the first date if they are looking for long-term partnerships.

Women need to be stimulated in all parts of their bodies to be aroused, not just the genital area, as males do. This is why foreplay is necessary. The energetic connection with her partner or lack thereof is often what makes an intimate encounter a turn-on or a turn-off. The two people need to "vibrate" at a similar energy level. It's like an energetic link—if they are not on the same vibrational level, there is no chemistry.

Emotion is "energy in motion" and moves the same for men and women. It flows up the energy centres, the chakras, in bodies. Stroking the body opens the chakras and causes them to link to the other chakras, causing the body to open its energy fields, resulting in the full-body, multi-orgasmic effect.

Women take a more lateral approach, simultaneously feeling and thinking, which contributes to a state of heightened emotional response. Therefore, what women often require from their partners is an expression and fulfilment of their feelings and sexual sides as well as acknowledgement of their personal arousal. When their loved ones do not address this, disharmony gradually creeps into the relationships; but when this energy is addressed, there is more awareness of the avenues of mutual fulfilment on both sides.

Now that we have covered what women need to feel aroused and why, let's take a look at how the male can arouse a woman in some detail.

Art of Seduction and the Actual Power of Love

1. At the foundation of prolonging female orgasm is the art of seduction. You want your lover to feel as if she's the sexiest woman on this planet; the more you draw out the seduction, the more she will respond.

2. Foreplay is obviously a highly important part of lovemaking, but before the foreplay comes mood setting. Women love candles, massage oil, music, flowers, silk scarves, strawberries, liquid chocolate, and intimate settings. Think about the location of your props.

3. Stroking a woman's entire body in the form of massage and gentle teasing is a great start. It will make her feel relaxed, adored, and sensitized. Stroke upward to raise her energy, and don't forget to touch *all* parts of her body. Start with a feather-light touch, then increase pressure, then alternate.

4. Your woman wants to hear how you feel. Tell her with love and authenticity.

5. She loves to be teased as much as you do, so keep her guessing.

6. Initiate a playful dialogue so you can communicate about how the seduction is going and heighten the experience. This dialogue can be in the form of spoken or body language. Listen and be aware of her responses to your touch.

7. Slow everything down. Make it timeless.

8. Make love with her as though it were the last time you will ever be together.

9. When you sense she's approaching orgasm, hold back on whatever you are doing. This is a sign that the seduction is working but also that you can take it further. Be careful not to stop too close to her climax, as you may tip her over the edge. You want to make her wild with desire, so take it to the next level, which is beyond climax.

10. Keep stimulating her in different ways to arouse and raise her energy. Allow her to engage with you but not for long. This is about her, and you want her to know that.

11. When your newly awakened goddess reaches orgasm, let her rest briefly, stroke her, and begin the seduction again! She will tell you when to stop.

12. Enjoy the bliss you have created and know what you give you get back! Climax precedes orgasm, so by slowly and continuously stroking her, her climax will lead to orgasm, and the next step is multiple orgasms.

13. Recent research has shown that when the coccyx is stimulated in women who have never been able to orgasm, they easily begin to do so and enjoy a wonderful sexual sensation. You can now have you woman reclaim this energy by simply commencing with a gentle massage of her coccyx.

14. You can also maintain this sort of connection on a conscious level without having sex. This is highly beneficial to do on a

low-energy day or any other type of negative day, even one when you received bad news. This is all part of the orgasmic effect. See: www.theorgasmiceffect.com.

15. By practicing this energizing method, which begins at the sexual level, you can slowly master this energy on a full-body energetic level, which you can switch on in yourself at any time.

16. Practicing this method will gradually enhance and stimulate all the cells in your body, which causes them 'to sing and light up', and you will reach ecstasy. At this level, your body is reenergized and filled with bliss due to this 'inner light'.

17. This blissful, reenergized state is ecstasy, the fire of internal passion. Some religious saints have claimed to achieve such states of consciousness. You can attain this state through sexual ecstasy and meditation, 'cosmic consciousness', when the orgasm reaches the crown chakra and consciousness explodes into a brilliant light a rainbow of colours is frequently seen by the person experiencing it.

18. You can reach this only when the chakras are aligned and the power of love is present, connecting the energy centres and igniting your light body on the inside. This dream, we intuitively know, is possible because it happens on a soul level, and we are all naturally connected to the internal light; we just don't know it consciously and mostly only suspect this on a subconscious level, which is where movie material of superpowers comes from.

By acknowledging the divinity in one another, we evoke that presence in the other and ourselves. This is the heart of all relationships, at a deeper level, where lovers are equal opposites of each other.

Benefits of a Full-Body Orgasm: For Males and Females

Women experience orgasms as the energy slowly builds in the base chakra and slowly rises to the sacral or the genital area. It spirals to her stomach or solar plexus, then further to the heart centre, sometimes continuing onward to the throat and top of the head. An orgasm leaves her whole body feeling tingly, energized, and buzzing on the inside for up to an hour. Women who can orgasm easily frequently continue to experience multiple orgasms in one night. It also means the orgasm can stay in the body into the next day. Ongoing orgasms can be addictive, especially if the woman is relying on her orgasm to feel good every time. However, this comes under another heading of sexual addictions, and addictions come in many forms, including shopping addiction, adrenalin addiction, and addiction to extreme sports.

The Reason behind Sexual Addictions

Sexual or any addiction can become part of a person's identity and associated with those who provide it. This can also happen in a marriage or in any relationship in which partners separate, so people who are more sexually active may resent their ex-partners without realizing they are simply after the good feelings they had come to depend on from their former partners. This is a common occurrence. Males love to watch porn, although it is rarely discussed, and people rarely wonder why this is so for males but not for females. Many males indulge in sessions in which they need the 'mistress' to tell them they've been bad or naughty and need a spanking or bondage. This seems to be the case especially with males who make money easily gambling or in the stock market. Money flows easily, and they don't make special efforts to earn it, so they feel that they require 'punishment' for their unwarranted pastimes; unbelievable but true.

Even though women may like to watch porn, it's usually in the company of their men, who may like the visual stimulation. Females usually don't need visual stimulation for sex as males do, and the reason males like the visual has to do with *the way women orgasm*. She feels alive and energized, which is what fascinates males, as she will have that feeling ongoing for an hour or more afterward.

When sexual fantasy overtakes feelings of connection, the feelings get lost and can sometimes turn into sexual addiction or just the urge for sexual release from ongoing tension. Hence the urge for seeking sexual release and frequently visiting adult services. Disconnection creeps up slowly and unnoticeably.

To Conclude: These invaluable techniques on seduction just need to be applied, yet most males have no clue and wonder where they went wrong. Porn has no bearing on the art of seducing women. Follow these simple methods here take your time, and all the benefits of successful fun evenings will be there for you easily with minimum effort.

Why Men Have Genital Climaxes

Males experience orgasm generally in the genital area only unless they have practiced Tantra for many years and have learnt how to channel their energy. Because of the usual genital climax males' experience, their energy stays in the genital area rather than travelling through their bodies, which is why males want sex soon after they have just had it. The nice feeling lasts only a few minutes for males, so naturally they want to feel it again. They want the experience to last, and visual stimulation such as watching porn enhances this elusive, short-lived feeling.

Since women's orgasmic feelings last an hour or more, women have no reason for the same stimulation and men do. On the other hand, because this feeling for males lasts only a short time, they are preoccupied with this feeling, which they imagine has to do with ejaculation, but actually, it's from the build-up of the feeling they get on the inside in the heart region before ejaculation!

As males process everything through their heads or their genitals, going to adult services is a common expedient way for males to release their built-up tension and, get the visual stimulation that gives them the good feelings they're after, though fleeting.

When a man learns the full-body orgasm method, he can have an amazing tingling through his body that gives him lasting power and increases his sensual and sexual performance. His hardness and sexual pleasure increase and he lasts longer, which is what opens up and prolongs sensitivity that leads to ecstasy, which has nothing to do with the visual as all males imagine.

When a man begins to channel this feeling of ecstasy through his body, the pleasure increases exponentially and leads him to a completely new level of sexual experience in which he gets to know himself as a deeper and more powerfully connected man. This intensifies his performance on other levels besides sexual and gives him a greater level of attractiveness that builds his magnetism, giving him that added sex appeal women find irresistible.

The Benefits of the Full-Body Orgasm for Males

When a male begins to realize that the fabulous energy of full-body orgasm is sustainable and within his reach every time, lasting for at least an hour rather than just before ejaculation, this opens up a new way for him to see his performance and his satisfaction. Preoccupation with adult services, gambling, pubs, and porn reduces significantly because he is no longer chasing an elusive feeling forever out of his reach.

Having the techniques under his belt, the male can feel less stressed and more relaxed about himself in his work and personal relationships, as performance is something he no longer has to prove. He feels it on the inside, and it's projected out, giving him the charisma that makes him attractive!

This joy factor gives him longevity as it lifts his energy to the heart level, the one method that never fails and gives him lasting power when practiced daily.

To Conclude: Sex seems to be substitute for many unsatisfied feelings we all crave; this is why sex is such a turn-on for most everyone. Learning the enhancing methods described here can bring the sexual experience to a new level of sustainable enjoyment.

Pathway to Liberation

A relationship is based on what is present between two people moment to moment, so when they tune into one another's subtle messages of the body, breath, and touch, they enter realms that bring profound delights to their relationship that begin to develop more gentleness, loving, and sensual play as they embrace more of themselves.

Intimate connections come from knowing your connections to your heart. The freer you are with yourself, the better your energy control will be. The freedom you feel after practicing the orgasmic effect techniques can further enhance your fulfilment and pleasure, which is ultimately a deep connection with your soul. Tapping into this connection is very liberating as it's the soul's true expression.

In essence, we are serving the god/goddess within, bringing into play and stimulating the innate love and devotion to the divine aspect in us all. We can travel the pathway of connecting to and awakening the divine aspect the god/goddess in us through sexual union, meditation and service. Reaching this union through the sexual portal involves freeing ourselves from addictions, dependencies, regrets, guilt, hang-ups, traumas, and other baggage we all carry, generally from childhood.

This pathway has been called the pathway to liberation, the way by which we become free of all entanglements of neediness. This has been the ancient pathway of monks, but it unfortunately became mixed up with personal wants and needs, and the pure power behind liberation slowly became veiled behind a mist of superstitions involving sacrifices. *Giving up our negative struggles and overcoming the lures and lusts of greed and all other negative traits is the real meaning of sacrifice.*

Relationships need not be power struggles, as they often are; rather, they can be ways of exploring and discovering sexuality as a connection to our creative life force. When we identify and practice this divine, creative energy, it becomes a powerful energy males and females can utilize in many areas of their lives.

Sexual Relationships and Tantra

When you awaken the god/goddess, you get the opportunity to enter multi-orgasmic, ecstatic realms of pleasure. Time stands still; imagine the gods at play, having all the time in the world and not rushed at all. This begins when you open yourself to honest emotions with your partner, who in many ways becomes your reflection, enabling you to express yourself truthfully and openly, without judgement.

Everybody's experience is different. Some experience full-body orgasm while others have a deep emotional release of tears, laughter, or emotion followed by immense pleasure. Powerful dreams are common for most people some nights after.

Sex is part of your energy and part of who you are. As you work more with all your energy, *you will start to feel more alive, even electrifted,* as many healers do. When you bring more of yourself to your relationships at home, socially, and in the office, you will naturally increase the success in all areas of your life.

Tantric sex involves more emphasis on how you can discover your orgasmic experience, allowing you to explore greater levels of sex and the creative life force, a powerful link to your inner power. Tantra is more about discovering than prolonging your ability and increasing your stamina. The orgasmic effect technique gives deeper connection between partners and allows them to enter realms of greater openness and ecstatic freedom. They can sustain this into the next day through the techniques, allowing the feeling to ripple through the body. Practicing the techniques takes only a few minutes a day and leads to more openness as the body relaxes and the energy flows more freely. This is the god/goddess energy the divine principle in us all; as this unfolds it enables couples to enjoy greater heights of sustainable pleasure.

Tantra is adhering to principles of yoga meditation, mantra, and rituals for experiencing pleasure in its wholeness. It's really about learning to feel pleasure in the whole of your body, not just in the genital area. Using the orgasmic effect method is an effective and easy way of gaining the ability "to switch on" the orgasmic feeling rather than putting up with a bad mood, a bad day, or bad news by spreading sexual energy throughout your body. Modern Tantra gradually awakens your spirituality, an inherent part of your sexual energy.

The orgasmic effect method takes you further, it teaches you how to use the sexual energy part of Tantra, to rejuvenate your energy in your daily life!

This allows you to have a passionate sex life, a healthy, vibrant life, and a healing relationship with your partner. It also enables you to feel comfortable with your body and opens your eyes to new dimensions and levels of sexuality, which include spiritual awareness of your partner's innermost feelings and desires. It will make you more present in sex, sexual play, and enable you to create a sacred, loving space and other ceremonial practices that incorporate sound and breathing. This awareness takes your body's centres on a harmonious, erotic ride that heals your emotions and wounds from past sexual relationships; it brings wonderful changes that enhance your life in many ways.

A positive relationship with yourself is the key that enables you to have a connection with your heart. This stimulates love, growth, and nurturing from within, which is how to maintain health. It's a force that holds your energy and acts as a rejuvenator for your whole system, recharging your 'batteries'.

The Principle behind the Goddess Power in Women

Through the practice of Tantra, a woman can feel a greater connection to the goddess energy that is part of her connection to the divine mother—a natural protector of life all women embody. This connection enables her to open a link so her partner can also experience this transforming power as sexual energy, enabling him to feel his god power within. Connecting to her goddess energy she experiences the higher power within her, which enables her to connect to heightened levels of expanded consciousness and feelings of ecstasy. This natural way of experiencing the energy of expanded consciousness can also be experienced by taking the drug ecstasy.

Unfortunately, the drug controls the individual by creating a dependency that gradually inhibits energy flow. On the other hand, with the sexual experience, the individual is in control; real power comes from the internal power source, and never from any drugs.

For a man, Tantra provides an opportunity to experience a deeper connection with his inner power and have a full-body orgasmic experience rather than just a single genital climax/orgasm. We all want to be appreciated and loved, and sex is a direct way of expressing this strong need in us all.

The practice of real Tantra is best described as keeping your intimate relationships *alive, healthy,* and *vibrant!* Tantra means enjoying or experiencing pleasure in a different way, where the whole body experiences the orgasm rather than just the genital area. What naturally follows with practice, is unlocking the secrets to your power through your sexual energy that lays dormant within you when its activity is confined at the sacral centre only.

This power is referred to as the serpent power when it is fully awakened, and as the sleeping serpent when the power is dormant (referred to as the snake in the biblical garden of Eden). The subconscious awareness of the latent powers dormant in us all is what is behind the real Tantra and why people are preoccupied with sexual experiences.

You gain greater sexual stamina from the balance and harmony this energy can provide you if you allow it to enhance your life rather than make it the centre of your life. When you integrate it in your life, you can accomplish a lot more on the creative levels.

Part of the delight of tantric studies is that you can learn and advance; your potential for energetic and spiritual growth is never ending. Daily use of the orgasmic effect techniques provides immediate results, and you will notice a tremendous difference as your relationships and lovemaking become enhanced in the first few weeks.

To Conclude: Tantra for a man provides an opportunity to experience a deeper connection to himself, which is the direct link to his inner power; this is very liberating and is the soul's true expression. Awakening the divine aspect the god/goddess enables a couple to enjoy greater heights of sustainable pleasure, the divine principle in us all. This has been referred to as the pathway to liberation in many Buddhist and Tantra practices. Connecting to our inner power frees us from entanglements of neediness and gradually empowers us; the more we acknowledge the internal power source within us.

Common Q&A from Males and Females Regarding Sex

Question from a male: When I had a threesome with two ladies, we were in agreement we would play equal roles with respect to pleasuring. But why is it when they say they want to teach me about how to please with more ways and means, instead of taking control, they want me to do everything for them? I didn't mind, but I thought they would tell me how to rather than letting me do all the 'work'. Confused.

Answer: First, women don't really know their bodies well sexually before they are thirty. Even then, most women don't really know how their orgasms work or how to activate them. This is why these days there are new words in our sexual vocabulary, such as "cougar," which refers to a woman in her mid forties to late fifties, by which time women have discovered what turns them on and have gotten past their sexual attitudes from past conditioning (unless abuse was present).

Older women generally know what they want, but unless they are with partners who want to grow and expand with them and get to know their sexual needs, these women are limited as males are far too eager to use sex for satisfaction and therefore are usually all about visual fantasy and not really prepared to stay and learn more. They want more sexual encounters rather than the learning part, which goes further than just basic preliminary thrusting.

It's a good idea to learn your partner's needs and ask her (or in your case, those ladies), how they feel or what they wanted you to do rather than wondering later.

Question from a male: I want to learn, and I have asked an older woman to "break me in." I'm a hot twenty-eight-year-old who has found some very hot older women but not sure if they want more from me than sex only, how can I know what they want? Novice.

Answer: A male has to want to learn how to keep sex stimulating and hold onto the connection even if it is with an older woman. Connection is no different no matter what the age factor for pleasing the partner. Having a good time is not just about how good the sex is, although it might start that way; the male needs to be connected with himself to keep it interesting, and this also applies to women. A woman may be hot, but that doesn't necessarily mean she knows herself sexually. To have a good time with her, you need to get closer to her and find out what her needs are and what turns her on rather than thinking about pleasing yourself.

This works better with couples because they want to take time with one another to explore and discover—not just sexual positions but how energy works, which is different from just the visual fantasy that fascinates younger, immature males.

Get your "rocks off" first, and when you're ready to explore further and connect with yourself more, then begin to explore the next levels, which will take you closer to the ecstatic realms.

Question from a male: We've been together for eight years. We still love one another, but the sex has become routine, and she's not as keen as before. Would learning new positions help? Who could I learn this from? Do I have to go to a sex teacher?

Answer: Any sex teacher will give you only sex lessons or breathing lessons, as with Tantra. Connection is what you need, and going to yoga is the first step here. You need to get to know your energy and how it feels outside the bedroom first. You can get Tantra lessons that combine breathing with meditation. Going into your deeper part is like exploring a cave. At the entrance, it might be fun to compare different sexual positions, but by exploring deeper, you will find treasure, and treasure is never "instant coffee"; you need patience and a caring attitude that comes from inside. Caring is energy, as is sharing, loving, nurturing, and giving.

Question from a female: My guy doesn't want to go into all that learning; he says he just wants it normally without all the fancy stuff. He's a good lover, but he sometimes gets bored with it, so I don't really know what to do or how to encourage him.

Answer: This is a typical example of disconnection. When a male is disconnected with himself, he is always after more women, more sex, or more sex toys. He will never find the missing link because he is looking outside "the cave" and not interested in exploring it. Unfortunately, this presents a challenge to most males. Exploring deeper into themselves becomes a problem because it is confronting, and they may fear that by exploring further they will feel powerless.

You might want to tell him you love him beyond what he may discover about himself or fear about his past. You may encourage him just by talking to him and introducing some things slowly. You can go on the internal journey yourself by taking personal development courses to discover who you are. That way, you gain insight on how to go to the next step with your guy slowly. You can then lead him until he starts to take an interest in what you are exploring.

Question from a female: I had a few amazing sensual sexual experiences with a lover who had studied Tantra and knew the special positions and how to use the 'tools' of sensuality. It was an unexpected encounter that started at his hotel room as a blind date. The first experience was memorable and ecstatic and a real sexual fantasy that you generally get only in the movies. It was exhilarating, so I naturally expected that each time we'd meet it would be similar or more exciting than the first time.

Instead, it all went downhill the few times we met afterward. He admitted he had several partners. Then, in another meeting, he was not fully 'present'. When we met again, I asked him about it. He said he had been thinking about going back to his wife. That's when he admitted he was having problems with his marriage. I don't know what to think about this whole thing now, and I feel let down.

Answer: This is another example of disconnection. For males, it's all about the fantasy, and they will go to any length for it sometimes. Unfortunately, at the heart of any sexual fantasy—especially if the individual is relying on it as a way of feeling good—is a deeply unhappy person trying to squeeze pleasure out of wherever he can get it. He will do whatever he can to escape depression or feeling inconsequential; he needs to please someone to feel he is worthy of feeling good about himself.

My advice is to not pursue this situation, as you will become only his prop. If a motherly type comes along, he will unload his burdens on her, making it her problem. Learn from this and stay aware; ask your lover questions about where he is in his life and what he is really looking for by being with you.

Unhealthy sexual relationships

These are when one partner has the upper hand where in some cases males have informed me that their partner had suffered some unfortunate abuse as a child. This doesn't show up in the initial stages of the couple's relationship but will always come up later in life.

When this is the female, she can be cut off from wanting intimacy and not willing to participate or initiate sexual interaction with her partner. She is likely to withdraw and find a variety of reasons as a way out of facing her dilemma. In this instance the Alfred Hitchcock's movie "Marnie" is a good example that exposes hidden agenda behind repressive behaviour. If you feel that this may be the case in your situation, it's a good idea to find this movie and watch it together and download from the Internet, if it's not available at the video outlets.

If this is the male who has had some form of child abuse, he may feel very inadequate as a lover and will try to comply with his partners wishes and sometimes will become 'a doormat' in the relationship where his partner may never be satisfied with either his performance or will find reasons to chastise him for minor things. This behaviour can become a dependency type behaviour where either partner takes the upper hand and plays the parent role within the relationship, or the victim as the case may be, either one is unhealthy. This type of relationship does not give the submissive partner scope to be themselves and instead to stay within the role of a 'submissive child' who needs to be reprimanded, told what to do and not listened to. See: Nan Goldin: "The Ballad of Sexual Dependency" http://en.wikipedia.org/wiki/Nan_Goldin

Understanding Tantra

Tantra is a unique spiritual system capable of resolving the mystery of being and its relationship with the world without mystery. Unfortunately, it has been caught up with many misconceptions and misguided beliefs, disapproval, and censure, including ethical concerns, misuses, abuses, and opposition of the "authorized" theology. Above all, centuries of long antipathy of Islamic and Christian beliefs have been against Tantra for quite some time now.

Tantra and Vedanta are two of the earliest spiritual systems. The many offshoots of Indian religions practiced today as scientific, technical, and spiritual methods have led to self-awareness, ultimate knowledge, and liberation. The practice of Tantra is really an inner journey, leading a person to inner awareness as a starting point.

Because it touches on internal power, it addresses what is behind internal power. However, the common experience usually drives us to quick attainment, and we can get caught up in the sexual part of Tantra only without realizing or wishing to explore its deeper aspects. We need to embrace the inner and the eternal to reach the sublime, which is accessible to us all. The eternal is tied up with our divine aspect, which eluded Aleister Crowley but most of us do not put in the time or effort it takes to cross this threshold; instead, we go to the easy preferences that are governed by religious beliefs, or hallucinogenic drugs.

Because of all the pseudo-religiosity and its taboos, prohibitions, suppressions, and fears, the dilemma of "this common mind" is that "it" lives in desires but detests them. "It" fears emotions, though in them "this common mind" finds its strength and source of re-equipping its energies and releasing tensions. Hence, it lives in sex, is born of it, and celebrates and promotes life through it, but it fears all its implications, so it fears Tantra, because Tantra venerates sex.

Tantra is still seen as somewhat of a spiritual cult, and for over 5,000 years it has been regarded as a philosophy but not dogma or a body of doctrines. It does not claim to uphold any standards of morality, although it is not immoral. Tantra is beyond "moral" or "immoral." The Western theory of sin, which overwhelmed Indian theology after its contact with the Western world, has never been the domain of Tantra.

It also does not deal with social or individual models or with "what should be." Its primary concern is "what is," a sincere and honest acceptance of oneself and the world around, the truth of the being. It is a spiritual science that examines our experiences with the material world and explores our spiritual and physical energies, methods to expand them, and our place and relevance in the cosmos—the ultimate ground of being.

You may now understand my reference to Aleister Crowley in the prologue; he crossed all thresholds and explored all boundaries in mostly unethical ways and threw constraints of religious narrow-mindedness out the window. He paved the way for people to open their understanding to new ways of perceiving sexuality and sensuality free of morality and belief systems. In Sydney Australia, we have Norman Lindsay, who became famous for his exploration into this world in which he painted and sculptured muses to extend the sexual into the fantasy of art and beauty. These can still be seen today at his gallery of paintings and sculptures. http://en.wikipedia.org/wiki/Norman_Lindsay

These are all variations on the theme of Tantra, explored in a variety of ways by Lindsay and Crowley and their associates. They got their names and reputations simply because they were ahead of their times and dared to explore a world generally unknown. When all labels are taken away and our sensuality is laid bare, we all aim for the same thing, to find and embrace our inner power even when we do come across beliefs or individuals who will try to impose their authority. Not knowing where it is or how to find it, we need to explore and cross boundaries into unexplored realms, even when we do come across beliefs or individuals who try to impose their authority.

The Tantra way does not subject itself to intellectual problems or metaphysical enquiries as does the Vedanta and other early traditions of thought in the subcontinent and beyond, perceiving the "being" and the world as "Maya"—illusion, unreal, shadows of the real, or things removed from their original identity. Tantra does not handle questions of why or whence; it accepts all actions as they are, transmuting them into inner awareness and further into a creative evolution; it transmutes all desires into the vehicle of transcendence and all energies into the ultimate means of liberation.

Hence everyone has a right to feeling whole, and no one has the right to stand in the way of an individuals wholeness, no matter how they may try to justify their beliefs or religious principles.

To Conclude: Tantra embraces all exploration into human sexuality and sensuality. Its insights are far reaching as all that has been imagined is embraced by it; hence, there is no judgement, and it remains an embodiment and crosses all religious boundaries and cultural differences because there is no dogma attached. *Sex Is Not a Sin: Tantra for Healthy Sexuality* is a comprehensive handbook for informal sex education and Tantra. For more information, go to http://www.exoticindia.com/book/details/IDG578/.

Chapter 5

The Energy of Your Subconscious

You can turn your deepest desires into reality by using a simple format and get the best for your life by recognizing that your subconscious mind is the "command centre" for everything. This method is unbelievably easy and powerful, and you can use it for relationships, health, and balance on all levels, including attracting abundance into your life.

Here are some common questions I've been asked and my answers to help you as I have helped thousands of others. I'm truly excited to share this with you.

Questions

1. Why can't I manifest more effectively or regularly?
2. Is this whole law of attraction thing for real, or does it work only for the lucky?
3. Is there any way I can get started and get some fast results?
4. I feel like dozing off when I visualize. Is there some way to make this more interesting and exciting?
5. How do I find my perfect partner? Is there a way of knowing how to?

Answers

1. When our own belief systems get in our way, we don't believe we have the power to manifest.

2. Regular visualization is how you start working with this law; luck has nothing to do with it.

3. Having a goal to work toward and work that makes your heart sing are good ways to get started. There is no "instant coffee" where your goal is concerned; perseverance is the key!

4. If you're not excited with the work you're doing, consider it your reality check. Find out what will give you that excitement feeling, and your visualising will take on a new meaning.

5. Sometimes people think they want a partner, but deep down they may not be ready, as they may need to take a break, or they could just be too busy. You may not attract the right person when you're not fully committed to giving sufficient time to your new adventure. Be sure you also have something to contribute to a relationship so you are not coming from neediness.

If you've ever asked any of these questions, even if you didn't want to admit it out loud, it's extremely reassuring to know you can make this work for yourself. Anybody can take these steps, the essential foundation for creating your life-changing visualizations, is the key for any personal goal, whether it's getting in shape, finding that perfect partner, or 'lighting up' your business. The science behind these five simple steps confirms how powerful the universe is when you become *a vibrational match to anything you want to attract.* It all comes down to how you use your energy. It will feel magical sometimes to see how things start changing and regrouping as your daily practice begins to bring everything you need into your life.

Your subconscious is the command centre that supports your visualizations. When you deeply understand how important saying yes is to everything you want in life and making sure you really want begin to work with your mysterious subconscious power and change the course of your life.

Your Greatest Results Begin with Your Decisions

Decisions, or the lack of them, are responsible for the breaking or making of any career. Those who are proficient at making decisions without being influenced by others' opinions are the same people whose annual incomes fall into the six- and seven-figure range. However, it's not just your income that your decisions affect; your life is dominated by this power. The health of your mind and body, the well-being of your family, your social life, and the relationships you develop depend on your ability to make sound decisions.

You can perform a mental exercise in a millisecond that will solve enormous problems for you. It has the potential to improve almost any personal or business situation you will encounter, and it can literally propel you on the path to incredible success. This mental activity is called "decision."

Those who are doubtful will become despondent and virtually incapable of productive activity. You can virtually eliminate conflict and confusion in your life by becoming proficient at making decisions. Decision-making brings order to your mind that is reflected in your objective world, your results.

How can you develop this mental ability? Quite simply, you must do it on your own, it's not difficult to learn how to make wise decisions. Our awesome power is subdued by our many distractions on a daily basis such as spectator sports and news tabloids that when we indulge in them, they rob us of our inherent power when negative images override our common sense.

By arming yourself with the proper information and by subjecting yourself to certain disciplines, you can become a very effective decision maker.

Negative images have been crowding your mind since birth. These come from negative self-talk, which is a generalized way of labelling them. The failures in your life weren't fault issues—you simply had no harmony with what you were trying to do.

> *If you fail to determine your definite purpose, everything else is wrong. Once you determine your purpose, you won't even have to think how to earn money; it will be as though an unseen hand is guiding you and everything falls into place.*

Nobody knows your gifts better than you do—not your parents, guardians, teachers or bosses, not even your best friends. Seek your own purpose. The world's masses like to lump things into successes or failures and are obsessed with conformity rather than creativity. You must seek your unique gift and not listen to the masses, as you are an individual, phenomenal expression of life, just as each flower and animal cannot be compared to others. You express yourself with your inner gifts that were there from the beginning, and they determine your performance from the "stage" of your life.

It's imperative you recognize what it is you're good at, what it is you really love to do. Your purpose in this life is to do what you love. When you truly start doing what you love, it's like being twelve again, waking up to your first glorious day of summer vacation. You're loaded with unique ambition and purpose and experience many things that will slowly draw you to your ultimate purpose. All you really need to do is be patient and adventurous, and your inner purpose will open to you and you will sing from the inside your unique song.

Look up "Self Help" at www.longerlastingmastery.com.au to find many practical suggestions on how to move forward and discover your individual niche.

Your Decisions Can Energize You

Decisions or the lack of them can make or break careers. Those who are proficient at making decisions without being influenced by others are the people who achieve more and have higher annual incomes. It's not just your income that is affected but your ability to make decisions; your whole life is dominated by its power. Your mental and physical health, the well-being of your family, your social life, and your relationships depend on your ability to make sound decisions.

Temper your decisions with discipline. The same concept works when a person decides to lose weight. If that person is offered chocolate cake, he or she wouldn't say, "Wow! That looks good. I wonder if I should …" Instead, his or her decision has already been made in advance.

When people withdraw from life and shut themselves off in prisons of their own thinking, they eventually find they are in a rut. This can happen when someone, for example, has met with failure repeatedly in spite of trying. Repeated failures can damage people's self-image and cause them to limit themselves and lose sight of their visions and faith in their potential. This is when they can decide to give up and resign themselves to seeing themselves as failures. Be aware of this pattern and try to intervene if it's someone you know you can help change their situation for the better.

The Difference between Saying Yes and No

I have met many people who say no to a lot of things without even realizing it, especially when they get older and are tempted to pursue something new. Even when opportunities are presented to them, they back out. It's a knee-jerk reaction; they don't try to see how it may not be that hard. Of course, many older folks use backup excuses, saying they don't have the money, but money frequently doesn't come into it.

Saying no can become a habit simply out of fear of the unknown. If you hesitate when you're invited to things, what excuse do you use as your backup, and do you choose only safe things? See what fears come up when you consider launching into a venture that excites you. What excuses stop you from pursuing it? What's behind your fear? Do you hide from taking action and stepping out?

Some people, in order to avoid any confronting decision, prefer to have a little sleep. Their internal mechanism makes them feel tired whenever they need to make a decision, or they will smoke a substance or get drunk. I asked a few people at a seminar how they coped with making decisions. One person said that when decisions come up and create stress, she would just go to sleep and feel better after but would still procrastinate with her decisions. Other people develop headaches when they need to make decisions. Such habits can trap people.

An easy way to overcome the negative habit of indecision is to become aware. Are you reacting to a situation, leading to a knee-jerk response, or are you responding, which means you stop and consider how you are reacting? When you take yourself through this simple way of inner appraisal, you will find yourself moving forward more easily, achieving more, and living out your dream.

Follow this simple list to identify possible negative internal dialogue to identify how you respond.

- Do you change or avoid certain subjects when they come up in conversations?
- Do you avoid having a close friendship with the person who encourages you?
- Do you use sleep to avoid thinking or making a decision?
- Do you feel burdened at the thought of changing directions to change your life?
- Do you take over a conversation to lead it in your direction to avoid an outcome?
- Do you feel burdened when you are asked for advice?
- Does an excuse come up for you whenever you get an opportunity?
- Do you find yourself reacting or responding to situations?
- What dream is still waiting to be fulfilled?

To Live Wholeheartedly Takes Courage – Security is mostly a superstition and does not exist in nature. Avoiding danger is no safer in the long run than outright exposure to it. Life can be either a daring adventure or nothing. What do you choose?

To Conclude: Living with positivity takes courage and can be affected by small steps. This encourages you to make more-positive decisions to move your life to greater satisfaction at work and at home and become more focused on things that benefit you in the long run. All it takes is to pause and ponder what direction you might want your life to take and explore the possibilities by asking questions and doing a course.

Ways of Regaining Your Energy

Frequently I'll ask a client, "Whom do you want be in charge of you when you're seventy or eighty? You, or a doctor or hospital?"

An accountant client considered that question, and I waited for him to respond for fifteen minutes. He couldn't answer the question. He wondered whether it was normal to anticipate that at some stage a hospital would take care of him since he could afford it. Subconsciously, many people believe it's normal to think this way and automatically assume this is how they'll end up.

I saw a documentary not long ago about how some tests were being conducted in London that focused on one person at a time who was living in the fast lane, clubbing, drinking, and consuming fast foods. The tests from one individual showed that his liver was that of a forty-nine-year-old male, his heart of a thirty- eight-year-old, and his kidneys of a forty-year-old. He was only twenty-six. There were several of these documentaries, and each week the statistics were similar.

We generally say, "Well, I'm nowhere near that bad," but I've met many executives who are busy meeting clients for business lunches. One lunch after another, the build-up accumulates and becomes similar to that of the fast-lane twenty-five-year-olds; the only difference is that the build-up is slower.

When people don't take note of their progressing habits and correct them early, the habits take over and the people unwittingly give in to internal dialogue that excuses them. They don't consider how their bodies have changed. Most people consider it a normal aspect of success, a busy lifestyle, or the pursuit of money.

Dropping Weight Fast Program

I take individuals through what I have called; a "Health Rejuvenation Program" where I teach them how to 'drop weight' very fast, that changes their entire way of living and seeing themselves. This natural method teaches how to maintain a regular weight just by following some simple principles of how we identify what foods nourish you and what are filler foods or plain advertising, and it works every-time because there are no diets involved.

A client walked in though the door recently and could barely walk his weight had swelled to massive proportions and would have tipped the scales at well over 140k. He said that he was ready to change his life. I always wonder how a person when seeing that movement is uncomfortable for them continues their habit without stopping to recognise that they are no longer able to tie their shoes laces, bend down or walk through doors comfortably. How they don't stop earlier to address their issues but continue their punishing ways of making their own lives difficult ?

If this is you, or someone you might know encourage them to see a life coach, or talk to this person because it takes a long time to correct the situation when it has gone out of hand and becomes a huge struggle that will take them best part to a year and more to bring their situation under control.

Some Simple Steps to Consider

Here are some simple steps to taking care of yourself. Start with tai chi or yoga classes—one class a week will start you off. You will see how it helps, and you'll feel lighter and freer, and the burdens will seem to lessen. I had a client who was very shut down and "cut off" was perhaps the best way to describe his manner. Many professionals get used to having this alienated manner. After taking up yoga for about a year, however, he became a changed man, more personable and more aware of himself and his feelings. He found a warmth that was previously lacking, and he was no longer feeling disconnected.

Yoga allows your mind to stop for that hour and gives your body a sense of relief, allowing you to connect to your mind-body intelligence and to find a natural solution to whatever you may be facing. Connecting to the human emotions and people in your life creates a natural balance that comes without effort. You will discover what is really taking place, and you will slowly begin to tune in to a much broader and higher level of information that resides within yourself, which is what mind-body intelligence means. This happens by simply giving yourself the time and space for that silence to gather and for your internal wisdom to emerge and present itself for any solution you need.

What Depletes Your Energy

When I go on walks, I frequently see many people, especially in their twenties and thirties, jogging. There's a beautiful cliff walk overlooking the ocean not far from me, and it's usually full of joggers, especially in the morning. When we jog, everything in the body is working at a very fast rate, including blood circulation, and many people think they can eat whatever they like and a simple jog or weightlifting program at the gym will keep their body fat down.

What people forget, however, is that whatever they eat gets broken down and circulates through the system at a much faster rate especially when they are jogging.

When they eat regular quantities of fatty foods, fast foods, and foods they know are not very good, and exercise or jog, whatever they are digesting is forced to circulate through their systems at an accelerated rate. This is why people may not feel very energized by exercising and put it off or get tired after it.

Be wise; consider what you are doing to your body long term, and be aware that people who are into fitness professionally eat very little red meat. Red meat doesn't give you energy; fish and vegetables do. What gives you real energy is when your blood is oxygenated, which comes from eating raw salads and lightly cooked green vegetables. Red meat weighs heavily on our systems and takes longer to digest because of the many toxins in it, including the adrenalin released by animals before slaughter, which is highly acidic and toxic to our digestive system.

Health Clues to Consider

If you feel uncomfortable as you jog or feel tired especially after dinner, what you ate may be causing the discomfort. Sometimes it's not very noticeable, but remember this rule of thumb: some foods will extract energy from your system while other foods will add it. Bread, meat, salty and preserved foods, sugary drinks, and fast foods extract energy. The more you eat these, the more your body needs to labour to process and eliminate them. Sugary drinks take energy away, so drink more water instead. Bananas actually give you an energy boost far more than any coffee would.

Another thing worth considering is that people who really want to gain stamina and muscle avoid red meat. Fish is a source of protein, and professional weightlifters who want to build muscle learn this fact early on in their training program. The biggest muscle-building foods are greens and fish. Arnold Schwarzenegger was quoted once saying, that one of the fastest ways to access energy was to eat quantities of broccoli daily.

Tips on Getting Unstuck

You've seen how people look when they're worn out from a conference, a demanding boss, or a difficult relationship at home. You can see it on their faces—they look drained and empty. To alleviate this feeling, they will go to the pub or sit in front of the TV, but they wonder why they feel tired the following day. The main cause of this dullness in people is being stuck in life.

If you're feeling stuck, not moving forward in a relationship, at work, or in a financial situation, consider how this situation will be for you next year, in ten years, and in twenty years. Looking ahead like this will give you perspective on the reality of your situation and help you decide what you are prepared to do about it now rather than continuing to avoid the situation, which gets progressively worse.

Here's a famous quote in personal development circles: *'Doing the same thing over and over and expecting different results is entertaining insanity'.*

People say, "If only I won some money, it would change all that," but if you have a mindset governed by a feeling of being stuck or of lack, it will not go away with more money. Money will alleviate a situation for a little while, but it will not eliminate a feeling due to unresolved causes. Your situation will only reappear if you fail to address the causes behind it, and you will be back to where you were before you got the money.

A Good Method of Getting Your Answers

When I want to resolve something, I make an intention of getting an answer by the end of a walk. In the beginning the mind chatters endlessly but as I start to breathe the air and enjoy the feeling of being alive, or remember some simple things I am grateful for the focus shifts, and by the end of a walk, a more refreshed feeling would replace the stagnant one, giving me insight on a new perspective on what I want in my life.

The 'TED TALKS' website features a diverse range of individuals speaking on many innovative ideas. Listening to any of the educational talks presented on this site will help you gain ideas on how to shift and how to produce some changes in your life (http://www.ted.com/talks/browse).

To Conclude: A habit takes hold of us unwittingly, especially when we are not aware of an internal dialogue that stops us from moving forward.

Taking care of our habits means learning to recognize how our energy is affected by different situations. Being aware of our internal dialogue will shift a negative habit and create a positive, new one. Taking action is the only way to move forward, seeing a health professional or life coach will help you initiate your direction.

Overcoming Loneliness

Do you feel out of sorts when you date, perhaps haunted by memories of an old love while you're with the new special someone? This is not something you can correct by reading books or talking to people. The feeling of loneliness, like all feelings, comes from inside. It's a symptom that all is not well inside you, and it's not one to ignore. As with weeds in the garden, ignoring them, thinking they will eventually go away, is ludicrous. Weeds might go away for a short period if you just pull their tops off, but they will come back twice as strong, because the roots will have strengthened. It's the same with loneliness, which comes from disconnection with your inner child. It is essential therefore to do some inner-child work and not delay addressing this important side of yourself. You can divert and distract your attention, but loneliness is insidious and will not go away—it can follow you all your life.

Being balanced with yourself and others is not something you are born with. The abyss of loneliness that happens after a relationship ends keeps you from getting back to balance with yourself and moving on. Sometimes when you're in between relationships, rebalancing, or grieving, the feeling of being on your own again can be very lonely.

The first step is wanting to heal your wounded heart. This is an important time to assess what is going on inside you rather than reaching out because you're lonely. If you feel tied up with a previous unresolved relationship, you may attract a similar relationship, which is what being "on the rebound" means. Reassessing your true feelings and emotions will eventually bring new connections with others, but the first step is to reconnect with yourself.

Wouldn't it be good to release past hurts and create positive changes in your life at the same time? To reclaim the life you were meant to live and have an easy method at your disposal that also helps you stay on track? When you have addressed this part, you will love your own company. Think of it as a wound needing attention, if the ailment is not removed from inside it will go on festering, bothering you, and never healing. The good news is you can heal it easily and permanently by removing the cause; that may be as simple as removing a splinter or sometimes it may take a little longer to address.

Here are some helpful tips to propel you to greater vitality and understanding in your relationships. You will discover how to find what you are looking for and why it has evaded you with these steps.

- Have a role model who inspires you to be balanced with yourself and others.
- Become self-aware of your responses to others, the key to achieving harmony in all your relationships.
- Set ten minutes aside in your day to get control of your emotions.
- Discover helpful CDs with simple techniques to help you stay in control.
- Decide to gain control of negative emotions.
- Read 'Homecoming' by John Bradshaw, an excellent and inspiring book on overcoming negative emotions from childhood issues. http://www.goodreads.com/book/show/12124.Homecoming

The link below also provides several topics to start you off on your journey to self-healing and reclaiming your internal balance and vitality, and healing your inner child. http://www.essentiallifeskills.com/store/

Reconnecting with your heart is a simple way to reconnect with your internal energy. By reconnecting with yourself, you will also reconnect to greater intimacy with your partner(s) and become an amazing lover if this has been missing for you.

To have great connection with another person, you need to have ongoing connection with your energy first. When someone you know and care about is stuck in past memories or has a broken or a wounded heart, a new relationship can be difficult. This new method will reawaken your energy as it gradually heals and allows you to connect naturally and easily.

An Exercise to Release Any Haunting Memory

If you are stuck regarding any relationship, this exercise will help you find a solution. You might need to make a decision now to follow this exercise here below, if you want some changes to and move on in your life. You will be amazed how easily this exercise can resolve some limiting beliefs about any relationship and provide you with ideas for further ways of solving sticky problems.

When you think about the words "haunting memories," consider where these memories are. You may agree they are in your head. (Well, they're not in your feet, are they?) Take just a moment here and come with me arm in arm (so to speak) to view the relationship or any past situation that may still be causing you painful memories.

1. Notice what you are replaying and where this replay is happening. Would you agree it's circulating in your mind?

2. Let's look at another scenario. Let's say the same thing happened, but this time to your friend. Would you replay the event as frequently?

3. Let's say this same thing happened to your son or daughter. Would you be replaying this in the same way?

4. Imagine this same scenario happening to someone you know in passing. He or she stopped you in the street and related a scenario. Would you replay that scenario endlessly?

It's very important to really pay attention here and complete this little exercise to get your results and make a shift in your thinking perception. Try to replay the same scenario, one after the other, from these four different perspectives, getting into the shoes of the others involved in the scenario.

Begin by setting up four chairs and draw simple faces on paper to make these situations more real. This way you can see it's not happening to you but to those you are viewing. Be very conscious how you view this now and observe if you are as engaged now as before. You must persevere if you want this to work.

If you are doing this exercise in your mind instead of setting up chairs with pictures of the people concerned, you can add some alternatives to this, such as brightly coloured hair, a long nose, and pointy shoes. Make the character of your 'past hurt' very comical and replay this scenario several times over, with slightly alternating colours, shapes, and sizes. For example, you could turn the character into a giraffe or rhino or hyena to make the character more outrageous.

For best results, repeat this exercise whenever you get into that mood and "catch yourself out" every time you begin to fall into your familiar trap. You will soon find that the underlying discomfort will slowly dissipate and that you feel 'yourself' once again, wondering how you stayed stuck for that long in that mood. It's critical to do the exercise whenever you have this feeling because you may wonder if it's totally gone. Repeat the exercise until the feeling totally fades like a mist in the morning sun. When you get into the habit of repeating it, it will take less and less time, and the repetition will become a simple thought, like saying no to the feeling you no longer wish to entertain. Your past habit will no longer have a grip on you as before. Yes, it works, but persistence is the key !!

To Conclude: Reassessing your true feelings and emotions after doing the ideal exercise to release a past hurt, will eventually bring new connections with others. When you persist with the exercise, it will reconnect you with yourself and create a shift in your perception and bring newness into your life.

Bringing New Energy into Your Home

Bringing new energy into your home can be as simple as bringing in a nice flowerpot or crystals to brighten a room as long as you don't add clutter. Here is a rule of thumb: before you bring any new thing into your home, you must take something out. This can be easy to do as long as you develop the mindset of automatic de-cluttering! This is essential to keeping your home or office free of stagnated energy, which can be very draining on your "mind space" and can prevent you from feeling inspired and progressing in your life. This applies to buying anything, including clothing and furniture. Make it a rule to eliminate an "old" when you buy a "new" so you de-clutter automatically.

Everything, including furniture and clothes, has energy. We walk into a room or someone's home and feel either comfortable or uncomfortable, and most times people will visit certain places or avoid others because of this factor, sometimes unconsciously. Good tip to bear in mind!

Tips on De-cluttering

Anything from a previous relationship, even clothes, will not give you the "lift up" feeling; quite the opposite. Life abhors a vacuum, so as soon as you've removed the old, whether clothes or furniture, you will have opened up space for the new. An opportunity usually comes up quite soon to fill that space, but first you need to empty that part, try it out. Hallways and walkways need to be free of anything that obstructs your daily energy. Remove it and your life will feel "freer."

Energy is movement, and some things need to move on, especially when they've been with you for prolonged periods. That's how you know it's time to de-clutter. This can be time consuming, but even if you have a busy life, you can do a minor spring clean once or twice a year.

Effect of Mental Stagnation

The feeling of mental stagnation is due mostly to disconnection. The "absent minded professor" is a familiar image of disconnectedness. I heard a professor once tell an audience of several hundred that for a professor, the body simply serves to carry the head. He was joking about how disconnected professors are and was actually referring to himself!

Most males I work with are totally disconnected from their feelings. The more disconnected people are, the longer they are usually in denial about situations in their lives and have avoided facing them. Disconnection is another way of seeing denial remember the play on words I used before – "like swimming in the river in Egypt D-Nile" it all leads to stagnation, and unfortunately over time it will gradually lead to physical illness. Bearing in mind emotion is energy in motion, hence even a blockage in a stream of running water will sooner of later lead to stagnation.

The Case of a Famous Brain Scientist
Releasing Blocked Mental Energy

Mental energy is our actively thinking mind engaged in something we might hold dear and keep going over. It could be positive or negative processing. We often forget that mental energy can frequently become blocked due to our being on one track all the time whether performing, teaching, or relating to friends.

Jill Bolte Taylor a Neuro-anatomist - a brain scientist who was studying the anatomy of the brain, and how the human brain relates to schizophrenia and the severe mental illnesses. Her personal experience with a massive stroke, experienced in 1996 at the age of 37, and her subsequent eight-year recovery, has informed her work as a scientist and speaker. The Time Magazine listed her work on "My Stroke of Insight" as 100 most influential people in the world and she received the top "Books for a Better Life" Award from the National Multiple Sclerosis Society on February 23, 2009 in New York City.

Her experience opened people's eyes to how stuck one can become. In her famous YouTube video "A Stroke of Insight," she claims she "had to have" a stroke to open her eyes to how her brain's left hemisphere was completely out of balance with her right hemisphere. It took her eight years to recover from her stroke. In a brilliant "TED Talks" presentation, this now famous scientist explains in detail how she recovered and how a spiritual insight opened her eyes to a new world within our psyche and the importance of our creative energy being balanced with life on all levels. View her spellbinding interview presented by Deepak Chopra at a presentation he gave in Sydney 2010 to a packed audience, if you can get hold of it. http://www.ted.com/talks/jill_bolte_taylor_s_powerful_stroke_of_insight.html.

On Dreams

Psychologists believe that dreams are our unconscious minds unloading in symbolic form and that they do not have any real significance besides being a way of reflecting on the day's events. However, dreams are far from that simple. If you cannot remember your dreams, you could be stressed, out of touch with yourself in terms of self-awareness and awareness of your spiritual journey, driven strongly by your outer self (your ego), or blocked because you do not believe in their importance.

If you remember your dreams, you are active and advancing on the psychic and spiritual level. You are in touch with yourself, aware and interested in the pursuit of self-knowledge and self-discovery.

Dreams are like inner motivations that produce pictures about outer events in our lives. They are the signposts that show where our inconsistencies occur. I refer to dreams as coming from the pool of the unconscious. You might liken it to being in a forest. For example, debris falling into the forest lake is part of the usual forest environment. Anything outside of that—say, a trapped animal falling into and decaying in the lake—would be outside the norm. It's a little like that with the unconscious mind; it will communicate images according to the situation at hand by presenting pictures that shed light on current issues. The images may be complex, obscure, and detailed so that we pay attention to them, but they can almost never be taken literally.

Language of Dreams

Dreams have their own language. The message to your spirit from your higher self is like a series of clues informing you how you are doing so you can arrive at the answers that help you do better. The more dreams you remember, the more information you have to work with and the faster you can progress, learn, and evolve, getting clearer understanding each time. The language of dreams is very simple and need not be complicated. Here are a few examples.

Water is a symbol for emotion, so it depends on whether it's a flood, a gently flowing crystal stream, or a deep blue ocean. Deep oceans will indicate deep feelings; floods of emotion may show up as torrid floods, and clarity and gentle feelings may present themselves as clear streams in your dreams.

Animals such as deer and cats indicate gentle ways of expression. If they're wild elephants and tigers, the dreamer may be undergoing very stressful, out-of-control feelings about a home or work situation in which they feel they have lost control and are being taken over and consumed.

A friend or place from long ago is indicative of the way you felt back then, a feeling that may be revisiting you, or a memory you want to go back to (if you feel that was a safe time back then). On the other hand, you may wish to resolve a situation from back when your life felt easier.

Being chased usually means you are not facing something in your life. When you face the scary whatever chasing you, those dreams will stop. Scary monsters can mean one of two things. The first possibility is that the individual is spending time in places that have unsavoury atmospheres, like some clubs, pubs, and casinos. The other scenario happens to children who are literally invaded by negative spirits, which also hang around clubs and pubs.

Please take time to get in touch with me if this is presenting a problem; it is very easily fixed when you know how. My Web site includes my email address: www.essentiallifeskills.com

Falling or Flying Dreams refer to our spirit bodies exiting our physical bodies during sleep; you can read about this in any literature on astral projection. Hereward Carrington, PhD, was a well-known British author and investigator of psychic phenomena. His subjects included several of the most high-profile cases of apparent psychic ability of his times. He and Sylvan Muldoon experimented with astral projection and out-of-body experiences and jointly wrote 'Projection of the Astral body' http://en.wikipedia.org/wiki/Hereward_Carrington

Falling in a dream simply means your astral body is coming back faster than usual and you are becoming conscious of this. As your astral body returns to your physical body, you can frequently experience a falling feeling; your astral body could even jerk as it "returns" to your physical body. Flying is similar, but flying is usually experienced when you feel joyful, and hence the experience is once again tied up with becoming more conscious.

We all disassociate from our physical bodies in sleep; this is how our bodies re-energize and why we will feel refreshed on waking.

Do Your Actions Create a Legacy?

Do you inspire others so they can dream more, learn more, and do more with their lives? If so, you are an excellent leader. It isn't what you have, who you are, where you are, or what you are doing that makes you happy or unhappy; it is how you get others to raise their thinking and consciousness that matters most!

Stand up to your obstacles and do something about them. You will find that obstacles haven't half the power over you that you think they have. Never let the fear of striking out with new ideas get in your way. See what you can leave behind in any form of contribution—writing, painting, any charitable activity, or helpful ideas to improve someone else's life. It's very gratifying and fulfilling for the soul.

To Conclude: Situations and dreams cannot have a hold on you without your permission. This is a fact! When you face your fears, they lose their grip on you and will end. Paying attention to your dreams can give you great insights into your life and will simplify matters if you learn the language of your dreams.

Waking a person from a Coma

I thought I'd include a few lines on this topic, as it does have to do with the subconscious and i feel it's important to know that this is very possible as I have done this on a few occasions. It's about the individual not making a decision about wishing to stay or to exit the physical world, so they are literally "hanging around". It's knowing the right question to ask them; whether they want to face their situation they are in all over again.…. However as with any situation that requires a professional, it's always best to ask someone who knows the best approach and the individual's circumstances.

If you find yourself or know someone who is in this situation, please email me so I can help the family and individual involved, as its usually the family that suffers most.

Self-Care

Personal health maintenance is any activity by an individual, family, or community that improves or restores health or treats and prevents disease. Self-care, therefore, includes all health decisions people make for themselves and their families to get physically and mentally fit. Self-care is exercising to maintain physical fitness and good mental health. It is also eating well instead of self-medicating. It is practising good hygiene and avoiding health hazards such as smoking and drinking. Self-care is also taking care of minor ailments, long-term conditions, or overall health after discharge from a health care clinic or facility. Individuals as well as experts and professionals who support self-care enable individuals to achieve enhanced self-care. Below are some tips for easy self-care methods.

Are You Living the Life You Deserve?

Sharing Self –Care and Support : This is crucial to enabling value and scope in developing countries, and it also plays an essential role in affluent countries, where people are becoming more conscious about their health and want to have greater roles in taking care of themselves. To do enhanced self-care, we need ongoing support. When we have greater awareness of ourselves and correct our households, we can extend this to others.

We can become an open community in which health care becomes health maintenance. It starts at home and is easily done with persistence and the desire to live better lives free of illness and heartache. This involves sticking to the same rules of health care every day. Below are simple keys to keep in mind.

- Be discerning in the health decisions you're making; discover what has evaded you.
- Learn to be balanced with yourself and others; discern truth from drama and how it affects your loved ones.
- Maintain harmony in your relationships; choose kindness over being right. Decide to be in control of your emotions; take up meditation.
- Use helpful CDs to help you overcome dysfunctional negative states.
- Identify negative emotions and practice awareness; you always have a choice.
- Maintaining lasting power in the bedroom increases your self-esteem and self-confidence in your personal life.

We are all energy beings, which means at our very core we are composed of energy. Our thoughts and emotions are deeply intertwined and have a profound effect on our physical and spiritual health. We can discover how the best possible reality can look and feel by envisioning what is most needed at any moment and receive guidance and tools that bring us the best choices and inspirations for personal growth.

To Conclude: Emotion equals energy in motion, which means that our conscious and subconscious thoughts and feelings are constantly influencing our physical realities, including our physical bodies. There are many realities outside the physical; it is up to us to explore what may be significant for a deeper understanding of our inner worlds even if this means exploring outside the norm.

How to Attract What You Want by Holding Your Vision

Take the first step in predicting your prosperous future. Build a mental picture of exactly how you would like to live. Make a firm decision to hold on to that vision and positive ways to improve, and things will begin to flow into your mind to support that vision.

Many people get beautiful visions of how they would like to live, but because they cannot "see" how it can happen, they let go of their visions. Knowing how you're going do something is a plan, not a vision. The magic ingredient in your vision and plan is trust, as trust is full of potential. The more you work on your plan with trust, the more you will build expectation, the main ingredient. By holding trust and expectation, you will magnetize toward you what you are holding and focusing upon.

There is no inspiration in a plan, but there sure is in a vision. When you get the vision, freeze frame it with a decision and don't worry about how you will do it or where the resources will come from. Charge your decision with enthusiasm—that's what's important. Refuse to worry about how it will happen! A line from an old Agatha Christie movie *Murder Ahoy* says, "Damn the torpedoes, Mr. Stringer. Full steam ahead."

Setting you Sights Higher – The Nik Halik Story

Try this simple, one-minute exercise. Close your eyes as you stand in front of a mirror and picture in your mind that man or woman who you think of as the successful relationship you wish for, or a winner and role model for what you are looking for. Open your eyes and tell yourself aloud the difference between you and that person?

When we expect wonderful things to happen, it's important to see them in the present rather than the future. Nothing is too good if we believe and continue visualizing it; that way, we can focus and allow absolutely nothing to hold us up.

A dream starts with a vision, and every great dream begins with a dreamer. There is a very good example of this with a dreamer who started dreaming when he was eight. He was confined to his bed for many years due to illness and would just stare out the window. He composed a list of twelve items he wanted to accomplish. He wanted to become an astronaut, also to have lunch on the Titanic, and to spend one night in the great pyramid in Egypt, and to be a millionaire before he was thirty, were just some of the things he had on his list.

Nik Halik now teaches personal development and has ticked off all the items on his list except travelling into outer space, (hasn't given up on that either). See his amazing inspiring story, and always remember you have within you the strength, and the passion and with patience and perseverance, to reach for the stars and change the world as Nik Halik is now doing, he has just turned forty. http://www.nikhaliklive.com/.

Nik Halik refused to be captive in his environment. He believed that if he didn't see things happening the way he wanted them to, he had to make them happen.

It isn't what you have, who you are, where you are, or what you are doing that makes you happy or unhappy; it's what you keep alive in your mind's eye and regularly think about. Be patient and wish to be adventurous, and your inner purpose will open up to you, and you will sing from the inside your unique song.

A good exercise to practice at least once a week is picturing some of the most incredible things designed by mankind you've ever seen, and imagine what you would like to design or produce. After all the space shuttle or a seven-star hotel in Dubai or a painting by an old master came about exactly in this way. The words that come to mind are "creative genius," which also applies to the Japanese woman who was commissioned to do the entire interior design of Burge Al Arab, the seven star hotel in Dubai.

Here's another little exercise: Who comes to mind when I mention "godlike compassion, caring, and loving"? Or what author's name springs to mind when you think about poetry, drama, mystery, fiction, or comedy? Your hands are no different from those of a skilful artist, architect, mason, or technician. Your brain is no different from that of a genius, a winner, or someone with strength and stamina.

Our hearts are capable of empathy for the homeless and starving, and we have the same hearts, as did Jesus, Gandhi, Mohammed, and the thousands of missionaries around the world. If you truly look at yourself from within, all those qualities are there.

Famous writers such as Frost, Churchill, Stevens, Wilder, and King shaped the world. Great athletes inspire us, as do Olympic medallists and rescuers during earthquakes and man-made disasters.

Stand in front of the mirror again and picture that man or woman you think of as a success, a winner, or a role model. Open your eyes and explain the difference between you and that person. There is no difference except in how you perceive yourself! You have the mind, the hands, the feet, the fingers, and the heart to be exactly what you want to be. The only thing stopping you is the person in the mirror. You have all it takes; decide to make the effort and picture this for yourself with daily intention and focus.

Understanding your lessons gives you insight into the circumstances of your life and the ability to recognize you can change your life. No longer will you let things happen to you; you will take control and make life happen! Write your list of things you want to accomplish and read it aloud at least once a day!

Make time to listen to and hear your inner voice; that way you will always stay true to yourself until you are in your eighties! That way you will be responsible for maintaining your health and well-being. This is the key to connecting with yourself and others and staying in contact with your central intelligence and inner core.

We have all the answers inside; we just don't give ourselves the time to be still and hear our inner voices that adjust and rebalance all in our lives.

Identifying Who You Truly Are at the Core of Your Being

If we truly identify who we are, spiritual beings having a human experience, we become more human. We all seek and attain balance from one another, as deep down inside we are loving beings. A powerful program runs us all; our task is to come to this realization consciously. When we do, we automatically seek balance in our lives and naturally want to help one another, part of our internal god-being makeup.

If we disbelieve this truth, we seek this harmony from everything around us and are constantly duped by our minds, believing we don't have it. This is brought about by false values and overly stressed competition on the outside of us.

To Conclude: Those who have found this balance tell us they no longer struggle as they did before, their lives become easier, and money flows more easily as well. This concept is the basis for the documentary '*The Secret*', http://thesecret.tv/ featured on 'Oprah Show' 2006 and woke many people to this inner secret.

This law of harmony and balance, the law of attraction, promotes personal health longevity and internal youthfulness often reflected in the physical body. Living with these laws, we become an example to others in our daily lives and see the presence of this harmony around us; likewise, others get inspiration from this peace-filled truth, which brings abundance on personal and planetary levels.

Chapter 6
Full-Body Orgasm

The orgasmic experience is very different for males compared to females, and there are many varied opinions about how orgasms work and how to make them better, more enjoyable, etc. Sex toys have been invented to give individuals and couples more sexual pleasure when they're not getting sexual satisfaction. I'm going to open the topic here based on what I have observed and the effects on men when they experience full-body orgasms and the heights it has taken them to without sex or any sex toys but instead through a sensual massage.

What Couples Expect from One Another—
"Looking for Their Other Halves"

When couples form a relationship or bond with marriage, they form expectations without suspecting this is what is occurring. It's important to cover this subject because looking for his or her other 'half' is something everyone tends to do at some stage without really being aware of it.

As a young boy becomes a man, he begins to look for his special girl, princess, or life partner and eventually finds her. He then expects everything he (hopefully) received in his growing years from his family—love, support, nurturing, and caring—will come in some form from his partner without consciously realizing he's expecting it.

Let's look at a young girl growing up and seeking her prince charming. She too without consciously realizing it expects he is going to provide her with all the love, caring, support, and more that she (hopefully) received during her growing years. Neither suspects the other might not have received the caring, love, or support from their family, factors they unknowingly seek from their relationship.

Such projection of expectations onto mates is common; partners will generally tolerate this for a while, but it will become a burden on them one way or another eventually. As one partner begins to lean on the other with neediness, the other partner will either bear the burden for a while, trying to cope, giving advice, and tolerating it, but eventually it's not his or her problem. Unless the needy partner takes responsibility for such personal lacks, the other will crumble and possibly develop back problems, neck problems, anxieties, or other illnesses because the major cause of illness, including cancer, is the feeling of being trapped. The partner could slowly begin to move away, and most males will go to adult services or form secret love affairs to spice up their lives.

This is not because the man intends to move on; it's because he does not know how to help whatever the situation he is in more than he has. Unless he has done even a basic personal development course by way of the 'Landmark Forum', meditation or yoga or attended men's groups, males cannot generally support issues their partners are facing. If they haven't solved their own issues, how can they understand others' deeper issues even with a loving bond? This is not due to lack of support but to unresolved issues that slowly become a wedge in the relationship, one partner tries to be patient until realizing he or she is not able to change anything.

The seeking the "other half" of themselves in other people has been the age-old quest that causes people to wander the earth looking for this lost part of themselves. To find it, one needs to accept their own love within nothing more, which is what they realise eventually that was there the whole time; as was written in a song by Cat Stevens long ago, "The Answer Lies Within".

How Females Experience Orgasm

When a woman orgasms, energy fills her body to the point that she feels energized, relaxed, and fulfilled for an hour or more. When women orgasm, they frequently "sing" the orgasmic song. The notes women release become higher and higher as they near orgasm. This is similar to laughter; the funnier the joke or experience, the higher the notes reached with the sound for most males and all females.

The same can be said for dancers, who frequently report that having a great time on the dance floor is like orgasm, a phenomenon that doesn't need to be analysed by scientists. It is something to be experienced, like getting wet in the ocean. What's the point of doing tests on how people feel when they get in the ocean and get wet? Just go in the water and experience it for yourself.

The same applies when a woman allows herself to feel exuberant and free and experiences an ecstatic orgasm. To experience an orgasm, most of the time a person needs to be able to get past constricting, conditioning beliefs from upbringing about what an orgasm or letting go really means. Letting go of the mind and conditioning and being present in the moment is not always easy, but when a woman does not have that hindrance, orgasms can be explosive.

The unrestricted energy can be found in children who are fully present in the moment, not analysing very much until they reach puberty; at that age, their energy begins to, divide. Part of it is in their heads, as they use their discriminating minds, and the other part is in their developing genitals, with all the emotions that begin to develop during that time of their lives. I have previously referred to this splitting energy as polarizing, which means that instead of the energy circulating through their bodies, as it did in early childhood without discrimination, it's now polarized or divided between the two opposite poles, mind and sexuality. This creates havoc in children during the teen years, when they undergo identity crises with their developing logical mind.

This is relevant to women's orgasms, because when a woman has not dealt with some hurtful memories from her past or her conditioning, it can play the same havoc with her as it does with a growing child adjusting to the new experience of his or her growing body. I am referring to women having issues here, as a large majority of women have experienced some form of sexual abuse or inappropriate interference or possibly an unprotected childhood, and they can carry this secret throughout most of their lives until it begins to surface in relationships, or during menopause if it hasn't been dealt with earlier.

Sometimes the puberty problem can become very difficult to manage for both adults and children, *and it can bring with it unknown dimensions, such as "psychic energy," which is intuition not yet under control.* Hence, when they encounter this new sexual energy but have no understanding of it, they react in whichever role it may have been demonstrated to them during their upbringing.

Labels that Imprison Us

For example, if superstition or strict religious beliefs suppressed awareness during upbringing, then this awareness may have been shut down or denied. This can also be the case with addictive parenting behaviours; if a young woman experienced this as a child she could repercussions that would play havoc with her emotional development and psyche. This becomes part of sexual energy, and may be called by names such as dark spirits or demons if the individual had a background of strict religious upbringing, it can therefore cause an individual to literally separate from themselves, developing a mind persona or "split personality", when they don't know how to deal with it.

This would be an advantage for psychiatrists to investigate rather than resort to the only means at their disposal, which is to medicate and label patients for any conditions they have no labels for. *Many such patients can be purely developing 'mediums' that are instead labelled 'schizophrenics'.*

With the now famous John Edwards and James Van Praagh and so many others who started out 'hearing voices' in their heads. This is normal for developing psychics or mediums until they can differentiate between the voices they 'need to listen to' and what in fact is just "static noise" like a broken telephone until the signal is clear.

See James Van Praagh:- http://en.wikipedia.org/wiki/James_Van_Praagh.

See John Edwards:- http://en.wikipedia.org/wiki/John_Edward

Male Genital Climax

The wonderful feeling that males feel at orgasm lasts them a few minutes at best, as a large number men I have asked all agree this is exactly how they feel each time. The energy does not get a chance to travel through and fill their bodies as it does with women. Men naturally want sex more frequently in order to feel this great feeling again. A woman, not knowing this, may call a man a sex maniac because he wants sex frequently, but neither realizes the genital climax feeling is not the orgasm that it is for women; nor does the man ever know he gets just the genital climax, which is the reason the feeling lasts for only a short time.

The elated revitalized and relaxed feeling that lasts for an hour or more is the full body orgasm that most women experience. Males are programmed to believe that ejaculation equals procreation, but they don't procreate each time they ejaculate. Because males have an unexpressed belief that the more frequently they ejaculate the more of a stud it makes them, it bears repeating here: this is what instead drains a lot of their energy. Even so males don't seem to connect this fact with how drained they feel afterwards, hence the prostate and heart problems in a great number of males.

Feeling and Energy Are Synonymous

When a person cries, the tears produced involve a lot of energy, so after a person cries, he or she needs to recover from that emotion. However, when a person laughs, tears flow effortlessly, and the person receives an energizing rise in endorphins. Again, no scientific tests need to be done on this phenomenon; it's common knowledge, right? The same applies to ecstasy. A person can be "touched" by awe by witnessing the birth of a baby, experiencing exhilaration, receiving praise, or watching delicate phenomena such as baby animals or a child's first steps. These experiences create tears, and we say we are "touched"— touched in the heart.

Women frequently exclaim "Oh my God" and touch their hearts automatically when anything amazing, ecstatic, wonderful, awesome happens, a gesture not seen with males, have you noticed? When confused or disbelieving or fearful about something, we touch our heads, where making decisions, planning, and organizing take place. Feelings of the heart, however, are not matters we can figure out in our minds, so when we are in love or witness something spectacular and try to compare it to something we know, we always 'reach' for the words. This is because words usually cannot adequately express any emotion, so we are reduced to trying to compare a feeling with a reference we experienced before.

Mind and Feelings Are Not the Same

People regularly say things such as "I just can't seem to find the words for it" because all their minds can do is make comparisons to references they have stored in their memory banks.

If you think of your mind as your tool, you will get a clearer picture of who you are. The way you "feel deep down" about people and yourself is more about the real you, not your mind. To get a clearer understanding of how our minds works,_reread the part in "Understanding the Principles of Your Power Source" in chapter 2, the allegory I described on the mind, the horses, and the chariot; it's a very good analogy of the mind and how it operates and also how it presents us with learnt and stored data all part of how our mind processes on a daily basis.

As the mind is constantly making comparisons and relating to something by analysing, processing, judging, criticising, and assessing, this makes our amazing minds, our tools, that operate within the law of relativity meaning; we always try to relate one thing to another. The more we wish to refine our distinctions, the more polar opposites we will choose as our examples. When we say black is opposite of white or hot is opposite of cold, we're referring to polar opposites. When we talk about shades of grey or warmth, we move away from polar opposites for clarification.

This does not apply to feelings, though. For example, when we experience awe, we don't compare that to another moment in time; it's an experience all of its own. Likewise, green cannot be compared to yellow; they are separate. We'll feel differently about yellow clothes, shoes, and cars than green or red ones. These are all different feelings we may have about the way something looks or feels, whether it's in relation to places we visit, people we meet, or great outings.

To Conclude: Males do not relate to their feelings half as much as females do (as seen in the simple "Oh my God" example above). Not connecting with their hearts as much as women do with their lateral approach, men seem to miss out on the spectrum that women have that gives them many insights into their surroundings and greater sensitivity to and empathy with others and the world.

Whereas men see women as a variety of shapes, sizes, and availabilities, which is really 'seeing with their minds,' women see more 'into their surroundings'. They exclaim, compare, and comment, and they are awestruck, involving their hearts. Hence, the constant sharing women do among themselves.

So, when it comes to dating, many men fall short, as there is not the forthcoming sharing from the heart about how to best interact with women. Instead of sharing with men friends, they will just try to outmanoeuvre or compete with them, which is all about mental manoeuvring; hence, men generally miss out on the companionship women have with each other because of the heartfelt connection that women have.

Orgasmic Effect Described

The amazing full-body orgasm experience is quite literally spiritual, and those males who have experienced it describe it as floating "on cloud nine"; their lives change forever as they have touched the divine consciousness within themselves. A parallel to this experience is in the movie *The Fifth Element,* an exaggerated sci-fi version that nevertheless demonstrates something important. It's the moment at the end of the movie, when the "alien goddess" is placed on the altar with the four elements: fire, earth, air, and water placed in four corners around her. The four elements trigger a powerful beam of light to project from her heart centre and connect her with the heavens because of her awesome power. The movie portrayed this power as a beam of light that connected the four elements with herself being the fifth element.

When someone experiences the orgasmic effect, a feeling rushes through the whole body that is frequently experienced as light and travels up the chakras or energy centres. The individual experiences it as a floating feeling that unfolds into a realm of light and bliss that fills the body with a blissful joyous sensation. Instead of this being a fleeting feeling, as is usual with males when they experience genital climaxes, it's an orgasmic experience that floods the entire physical emotional and mental body and is present for at least an hour. This experience is easily available to males through the practice of full-body orgasm, which is what the 'orgasmic effect techniques' are all about.

Some have described this feeling as elation and expansion. As this feeling begins to flood the body, those who experience it feel they tower over everything. At other times those who experience it feel as though their feet are not touching the ground and their heads are higher than the building they're in, and the body feels so light that they just don't want to open their eyes. There are many descriptions of this ecstatic experience. Some say the spiritual body has expanded beyond the dimensions of the city, sometimes even the planet. Shirley MacLaine writes about this in her books *'Dancing in the Light'* see below, and her book *'Camino'* see below. http://www.goodreads.com/book/show/1121580.Dancing_in_the_Light http://shirleymaclaine.com/shirley/books-camino-intro.php

The Camino is the pilgrimage to the Cathedral of Santiago de Compostela in Galicia, north west Spain, where legend has it that the remains of the apostle, Saint James the Great, are buried. The Way of St James pilgrimage has existed for over a thousand years. It was one of the most important Christian pilgrimages during medieval times. It was considered one of three pilgrimages on which a plenary indulgence could be earned. (the others are the Via Francigena to Rome and the pilgrimage to Jerusalem).

The recent movie *The Way* depicts this famous and great walk with the many adventures everyone who does this walk encounters. Many people who do the walk end up having life changing experiences and/or healings.

How Relying Drugs or Sex Disconnects You from Feeling

Many people take drugs to find an easy way to experience ecstatic states of consciousness and find that illusive ecstasy our souls know is within our reach. A nice holiday will give you a little glimpse into this feeling; people usually don't want to return from a holiday because they have simply let go of all their thoughts and concerns of daily life and don't look forward to returning to it all.

The key words here are *letting go*. Sex is considered the most common and quickest way of letting go. But is it? For some people it is, and the better their orgasms the more they are able to let go. Sometimes, however, they cannot let go and need sex toys to stimulate themselves so they can let go. Generally, however, this occurs only in the genital area, and it becomes tantalizing for males, who make it into a sexual fantasy, and the feeling changes from ecstatic to indulgence. This can become addictive when people cannot relate to the great feeling any other way besides sex. They'll go to great lengths to get the feeling back. This is addiction and does not refer to sex only but to anything that gives people a buzz that they will over-indulge in.

A good way to make the distinction between a real connection and just a sexual one is this: if you use only your visual criteria for your sexual experience, you are most likely not connecting with your heart but to your mind. In which case, you are practicing disconnection all the time while engaging in this type of release.

> It's very important to make this distinction, as practicing disconnection is at best unhealthy and leads to withdrawal on many levels.

Why Males Generally Chase Sex

Males are always hoping to find "the right one" who will give them "the" experience rather than learning how to activate this feeling in themselves, thereby gaining control of it and the ability to fill up on it at will. This is the orgasmic effect, in which the energy slowly rises from the base chakra to the sacral centre chakra and then to the solar plexus chakra, the heart chakra, the throat chakra, the third-eye chakra or brow chakra, and the crown chakra. The sensation is a spiral that slowly pulsates as it rises. This is what I have previously mentioned when women sing the orgasmic song as the Kundalini energy begins to rise up the spine.

Yoga books and Indian tantric practices refer to this. The Kundalini energy rising up the chakras is the serpent power that travels up the spine. Church traditions interpreted this as a snake going up a tree in the Adam and Eve story. This was hidden knowledge; in the past, experiencing ecstasy through sexual practices was forbidden, so this knowledge had to be translated into allegorical, symbolic terms over 2000 years ago.

Adam and Eve are the masculine and feminine aspects within us, as referred to in the ancient scriptures from the 'Vedas' predating Biblical scriptures. The tree of life is the spine, and the apple is the fruit of knowledge experienced when you transcend your mind and merge with your spirit body, experiencing ecstasy. This ecstasy in turn is what gives you enlightenment, which is the fruit of knowledge. It is easy to see how this interferes with church doctrine, which does not accept the experience of ecstasy via sexual experience without the church having control over it. Sex was turned into a story and made out to be a sin, as told in the Adam and Eve story that was really an allegory about the awakening of the inner divine nature in every human being. Little wonder Aleister Crowley's works had a huge influence on stifling Victorian traditions that "needed to be" disrupted.

Individual's Orgasmic Experiences

Below is a description of such an experience a client had; he was changed forever, as it opened him up to his greater dimension of himself. After the massage, his third eye opened, he could not get up; he felt he was not in his body. He didn't want to open his eyes, as his spiritual body had "expanded" beyond his physical form, causing him to feel he'd become a giant and was taller than the six- storey building he was in. This made him feel he could barely put one foot in front of the other when he stood up. Below is what he emailed to me about his experience.

Hello, Tatiana. I would just like to say thanks for the overwhelming experience that I had. I am still trying to come to terms with it all and fully understand it and get my head around it all ahahhh! But it is awesome to think that one can leave one's body and be in "another world" realm or dimension or something. I did not think it was possible for a man to disconnect his self from "his Joystick" at the same time.

I have not told anyone about my experience, but I will tell my wife soon when the time is right once I have mastered the techniques that you taught me, which will take time and practice. I cannot get the picture of the "giant" feeling out of my mind when I felt so enormous. Funny, huh? And amazing!

My response was:-

Hello, Desmond. Yes indeed, the experience is something I will use as an example of what is possible for men. I have been to that place as you have; hence, I knew how to talk you through it and what was happening for you. It's best not to try to get "your head around it" as it's not for your head but for your heart.

You didn't disconnect from yourself you disconnected from your ego and left your physical to expand into your higher consciousness, which is a magical experience when it happens for the first time.

Continue connecting to that feeling; this is critical for you to keep the memory alive and reconnect to the experience with your higher self that you can now do each time again.

Google "Deepak Chopra," a medical doctor who has written many books on the spiritual path; Louise Hay, who is famous for her *Heal Your Life* book translated into many languages; and have a read of Eckhart Tolle's *Being Yourself.* They are world-famous spiritual leaders in their fields.

My Orgasmic Experience

I will include an orgasmic experience I had in my thirties. I clearly remember that day. I was engaging in a "dutiful sexual performance" with my then-husband and really didn't want to "be there." As a result, right in the middle of it I began to "talk" to the great masters of wisdom and saw them in my mind's eye as sitting and communicating with each other in a forum-type setting. I felt myself trying to get their attention through a heartfelt prayer connection; the best way I can describe this was, doing this through my crown chakra.

As I began to orgasm, because my focus was on my crown and not my genitals, the orgasmic feeling surged through my body. I felt as though my body had lit up with an astonishing brilliant light, and then I saw all the colours of the rainbow cascade through my body. My then-husband had no idea what was happening; I told him to leave me so I could continue to feel how the vibrations continued to pulsate within me.

On several other occasions, I had visions of sexual experiences—sexual rituals I never saw on TV or read about—and these visions would come only during a heightened orgasm. I'd see these visions on many occasions. For this reason, I knew exactly what my client was experiencing and how to guide him.

How to Activate Your Orgasmic State

The best way to get to this amazing feeling, and experience it regularly rather than rarely is to practice. If you wish to have an easier flow of energy and be stress free and energized at the end of the day, you need to spend a little time plugging into your orgasmic energy, preferably before you have breakfast or go to work.

The reason I have repeatedly mentioned yoga here is that doing yoga or tai chi you are letting go of your mind which frees up your inner being to emerge and enlighten you by gradually connecting you with your core, your true self. Artists and creative people are more connected with their inner beings and therefore inspired through this connection from where all ideas flow, which is a connection to this energy in another form.

When we come to that precious moment, we can experience this special feeling, which can overwhelm us with tears. Winning a big prize or getting praised as I have mentioned before may bring on this feeling, but these are usually fleeting moments. With some practice, however, we can plug into our energy via any of these avenues and gradually get to know this feeling easily and have this feeling on call. That's when we can be in control of our health, vitality, and overall well-being and experience speedy recovery from illness.

I have spent a bit of time on the subject of disconnection, because of how it prevents you from getting in touch with your very precious healing energy, that gives you all these benefits, which is the recipe for staying connected with your inner vitality. Your overall wellness comes from here, which is within your heart centre the source of your energy. Doing meditation at least once a week is key to connecting with your main power your heart chakra that maintains all your energy connections.

Why is all this necessary? The answer is simple. I always ask my clients, "If you were to injure yourself and needed to go to the hospital, or you became debilitated in some way, hopefully you would soon come home to recuperate. But who is healing that part of your body? Do you know how to mend your cells so they heal properly, mend in every part, and strengthen without infection? Do you know how this is done internally?" The answer of course is no. No one knows the process of how the body mends itself. So wouldn't it be wise to get in touch with that internal intelligence that takes care of us on all those levels automatically?

The next question would be: what is the internal central intelligence? This was covered two thirds of the way down in Chapter Two where central intelligence is explained in detail. See also in the Prologue under the heading of; "Our Divine Selves".

How We Can Stimulate Our 'Prolactin Immunity' Levels Naturally

Getting access to the core of our being is not instant coffee. We must first strip off our egos, the part of our mind that is our reference to the world, but the world takes no part in our inner healing process. When people become ill, even doctors will generally advise them they "need a holiday," they need to get away from … what? From the familiar daily thinking and repetition, which has no soul. People love holidays because holidays give them a "break."

Unfortunately, we constantly disconnect with our internal intelligence just as we disconnect from love and constantly need to be reminded. A practical guide for more information on Central intelligence, how to use it on all levels, is in my E-Book; *Energy without Drugs*. See :Immunity http://www.essentiallifeskills.com/store/

Below is an excellent site to discover how this intelligence works with what doctors describe as oxytocin, a topic Deepak Chopra discusses in his book *Perfect Health*. Also on the website "TED Talks" is an excellent scientific info link that proves what love actually does for us humans (Paul Zac, "On Trust, Morality, and Oxytocin," "TED Talks," http://www.wimp.com/trustmorality/).

A client of mine from the medical profession gave me his opinion from his medical perspective in an email to me on prolactin:

Sex has been and is constantly studied by both men and women. Research shows that during ejaculation, men release a cocktail of brain chemicals, including nor epinephrine, serotonin, oxytocin, vasopressin, nitric oxide (NO), and the hormone prolactin. The release of prolactin is linked to the feeling of sexual satisfaction, and it also mediates the "recovery time" that men are well aware of—the time a guy must wait before "giving it another go." Studies have also shown that men deficient in prolactin have faster recovery times.

Prolactin levels are naturally higher during sleep, and animals injected with the chemical become tired immediately. This suggests a strong link between prolactin and sleep, so it's likely that the hormone's release during orgasm causes men to feel sleepy.

(Side note: prolactin also explains why men are sleepier after intercourse than after masturbation. For unknown reasons, intercourse orgasms release four times more prolactin than masturbatory orgasms, according to a recent study.)

Oxytocin and vasopressin, two other chemicals released during orgasm, are also associated with sleep. Their release frequently accompanies that of melatonin, the primary hormone that regulates our body clocks. Oxytocin is also thought to reduce stress levels, which again could lead to relaxation and sleepiness.

It's clear from this explanation that science suggests it's all about how much prolactin the body is producing, how this influences sleep, and how other chemicals in the body play a part in regulating it. There is no mention of whether any of these chemicals influences a male to feel more relaxed or less stressed. The medical community says nothing about the prolactin we release simply by practicing relaxation or meditation or controlling these levels at will?

There is no suggestion that the above chemicals randomly doing 'their own thing' have anything to do with a man's ability to "last longer," but by simple practice, these levels will rise in a man's body because he is in a state of arousal. Therefore, the longer he can sustain this, the more the prolactin level will naturally rise, not the other way around. Chemicals have no mind of their own; our emotions in combination with our state of mind, however, will influence the levels of these chemicals.

Sexual energy is not all about how long you last in bed; it's about being able to convert and use sexual energy during the day as well, which is the whole point of this book. A male on average will fantasise, think about, or want sex up to a hundred times a day, as many males have told me. This build-up is not just about the tension on the inside; it builds up slowly in males just by looking at sexy females. As sexual energy builds, it stays in the genital area, hence the constant fantasising and thinking about sex. When this energy accumulates tension and has nowhere to go, males release it with masturbation as a quick fix.

However, ejaculating several times a day, as many younger males do, only drains them more, and by the time a man is in his mid thirties, he feels the effects of sexual release by feeling more and more drained; this increases the older he gets. As a male gets older, the sexual opportunity lessens, but not the stress levels, hence the expression "I need to get my rocks off." Males have set up a default system relying on sex to release tension, which only sets up a vicious cycle of build-up and release.

When males begin practicing getting their energy to flow through their bodies as is described throughout this book, they additionally gain control of their prolactin levels, and there is not the usual tiredness, associated with energy accumulating and being drained or exiting the body at ejaculation. Thus a male can train his body to reverse the accumulating energy, so his energy now moves through the body, which is how is works with women who have full-body orgasms. Women do not feel the drained after effect and are not sleepy as males are, so there is more to the prolactin theory than is concluded medically.

This is where the changes of energy levels occur when practicing the techniques; males begin to last not just for a few minutes longer but for as long as they want to. This lasting longer is the effect of practice that gradually increases and balances the daily prolactin levels throughout the body, which plays a big part in bringing stress down thus releasing more energy as a result. This is the breakthrough!

Science does the entire thing in reverse; it considers the prolactin and chemical levels in the body as separate from how a person feels. Science has not understood that *chemicals are produced in response to how a person feels* not the other way around, and that the chemical levels are produced in accordance with the fluctuating highs and lows of how the individual feels on a particular day. How a person feels will consequently influence the levels of these chemicals. This is logical, as when a person is stressed, he or she will produce different levels of chemicals. Conclusive tests have actually been done that show changes in blood occurring that relate to high stress levels!

Looking for the Missing Link: Cause and Effect

The above discussion demonstrates how doctors in general have not been trained to consider energy and see it only from the perspective of chemical reactions and the labels they have been taught to put on ill health; they reach for prescriptions, which are really a mixture of chemicals as a way of fixing a health issue. They do not believe it can be influenced by our own feelings and thinking patterns that are at the core of all our positive and negative experiences. However in a recent scientific breakthrough this missing link will now need to be considered by the rest of the scientific community, to look at the causes behind the very effects the body produces that underlie the illnesses they try to find cures for.

Looking at the full picture of causes behind every situation is the first approach behind any train or plane crash investigation. A team of specialists put huge effort into assembling the pieces to discover the causes behind the crash and to uncover what went wrong and how to avoid such an incident in any future flights.

This should be the first priority on the list with doctors to look at possible causes behind their patients illness, instead doctors are trained to look only at the symptoms without looking at their causes.

The greatest beneficiary and supporter of this missing link between good health and wellness is the pharmaceutical industry, which exploits illness and benefits greatly by keeping people addicted to prescription drugs. Every doctor is aware of this, as early in their training they are seduced by holidays and many study aids to keep them constantly reminded that drugs are very necessary and that there is a drug for everything. There is never any mention of how best to maintain health; it's always about the fastest way to medicate patients.

Drug companies are in the business of monitoring the effects of their drugs only to see how well patients can stay on the prescribed drugs; they are not in the business of healing any illness. This is the sad truth not known to people in general.

Amazing Scientific Breakthrough

The good news is that the scientist and biologist Bruce Lipton has spoken to a packed audience about his research discovery with stem cells, about this very question of the causes, that operate behind the structure of our own cells. *That we are not defined by our genes, as was previously thought for many years;* instead our environment influences our internal information within our cell structure. This was a huge breakthrough for the scientific community. Scientist and physicist Tom Campbell teamed up with Bruce Lipton and discovered they had come to the same conclusion from different scientific perspectives, and this led them to discovering metaphysical truths that are the basis and support of all life. Meta refers to the higher levels of anything.

This is great news indeed, and we can only hope that the drug companies are not going to try to squash this as they have done before by taking the herb comfrey off the market and prohibiting its sale in herbal shops; comfrey had health benefits and could promote healing in many areas for our benefit.

Bruce Harold Lipton (http://en.wikipedia.org/wiki/Bruce_Lipton) is an American developmental biologist best known for promoting the idea that genes and DNA can be manipulated by a person's beliefs. He teaches at the New Zealand College of Chiropractic (http://www.youtube.com/watch? v=HVECAlT4AXY).

Dr. Bruce Lipton with Gregg Braden from 'HeartMath and Global Coherence Initiative' presented this information and spoke on this topic at a conference in Sydney early 2013.

Bruce Lipton's breakthrough is about how stem cells are influenced by our environment not by our genes. Unfortunately this information has not yet reached people in general and some including film stars are doing damage to themselves by using the belief that their parents gene that was predisposed to cancer will also affect them in the same way. In order to avoid cancer they then have the mastectomy operation removing their breasts, as a result of this now outmoded scientific belief.

Medicinal Uses of Comfrey

Comfrey's healing benefits have been known since ancient times. Dioscorides, author of one of the oldest herbal texts, *Materia Medica* of 50 AD, prescribed the plant to heal wounds and broken bones. Many writers since have honoured the herb. The name "comfrey" is believed to come from Latin "confera," meaning "knitting together." The genus name "symphytum" means "to heal together, and comfrey is renowned for its ability to assist the body to heal any torn or broken part. This explains another common name for it, "knitbone." Leaves or roots of comfrey applied as a wash, poultice, or ointment are used for bruising, sciatica, boils, rheumatism, neuralgia, varicose veins, *bedsores, wounds, ulcers, insect bites, tumours, muscular pain, pulled tendons, gangrene, shingles, and other dermatological conditions. A grandmother told me she makes comfrey ointment so renowned for healing that her grandchildren call it "Grandma's magic cream." Adding comfrey to the bath water is said to promote youthful skin.

Comfrey acts as an emollient and is very soothing, inhibiting further damage to tissues and stimulating the production of cartilage, tendons, and muscles. It has been esteemed as a blood, bone, and flesh builder. Its leaves' dark-green colour indicates the richness of chlorophyll with a molecular structure closely resembling our blood. Chlorophyll acts as a catalyst that promotes healing in humans and animals and is a valuable blood purifier.

Scientific research shows that chlorophyll helps to rejuvenate old cells and promote the growth of new cells. This action, together with comfrey's allantoin properties (a cell proliferant), provides us with a very powerful herb. Allantoin is one of the elements that makes comfrey unique. It is also produced in the allantois gland of the umbilical cord (the link between mother and developing baby) for promoting rapid cell growth. Mothers' milk is also rich in allantoin, which stimulates rapid growth of the new baby, and then the element fades out. This process also takes place in other mammals. Allantoin is a leucocytosis promoter (it increases white blood cells) that helps establish immunity to many infectious conditions.

Comfrey has been used for indigestion, stomach and bowel problems, excessive menstrual flow, hoarseness, periodontal diseases, bleeding gums, thyroid disorders, diarrhoea, gastrointestinal ulcers, hernia, glandular fever, coughs, lung conditions, haemorrhaging, cancer, catarrh, anaemia, sinusitis, lupus, lowering blood pressure, hiatal hernia, and blood purifier. It can also ease inflammation of the joints and mucus membranes.

Comfrey was one of the most popular and widely used herbs of the last two centuries; people had faith in the plant, used it, and experienced miraculous healing. It was held in such high esteem that it was believed even wearing or carrying it could protect a person. I have more books on comfrey than any other herb.

H. E. Kirschner, MD, in his book, *Natures Healing Grasses*, devotes four chapters to comfrey and says, "A leaf a day keeps illness away." In his practice, he witnessed healing of obstinate ulcers, malignant growths, and many other ailments. He tells the incidence of an asthmatic man who casually nibbled a comfrey leaf when walking in a friend's garden. That night he had unbroken sleep, and when wondering why, he thought it could have been the comfrey leaf. He started eating a comfrey leaf a day and did not suffer from asthma since. He shared this folk remedy with many other asthmatics, and they also experienced relief.

Over the years, I have met many people who attribute miraculous virtues to comfrey and shared their experiences. The healing benefits of comfrey have been spread by word of mouth. There is no doubt the plant is very much loved and revered (http://herbsarespecial.com.au/free-herb-information/comfrey.html).

The Drug Companies' description of Comfrey

Comfrey (*Symphytum officinale*) has been used on the skin to treat wounds and reduce inflammation from sprains and broken bones. Comfrey roots and leaves contain allantoin, a substance that helps new skin cells grow, along with other substances that reduce inflammation and keep skin healthy. Comfrey ointments were often applied to the skin to heal bruises as well as pulled muscles and ligaments, fractures, sprains, strains, and osteoarthritis.

In the past, comfrey was also used to treat stomach problems. However, the 'drug companies have discovered' a substance called pyrrolizidine alkaloids that in 'large quantities' is toxic to the liver. The U.S. for this reason the Food and Drug Administration no longer allow any oral comfrey products to be sold in the United States. The United Kingdom, Australia, Canada, and Germany also have banned the sale of oral products containing comfrey. However people through the ages have drunk comfrey tea several times a day with no ill effects,

The "dangerous substances" in comfrey are also absorbed through the skin, and harmful amounts may build up in the body. You should be careful if you use an ointment containing comfrey (see "How to Take It" section in website below), and you should never use it on broken skin (http://www.umm.edu/altmed/articles/comfrey-000234.htm#ixzz2DvqLjte1).

However herbal ointments of comfrey were sold liberally in health food shops until the drug companies discovered its healing properties and then exaggerated their findings until they took over and banned the use of comfrey with all its benefits.

Unnecessary Energy Drain

How many males compared to females have triple bypass surgery, perhaps a hundred to one? Men without knowing it, constantly waste energy via the genital area as accumulated stress, and no one tells them any different. Every man will tell you as soon as he releases sexual tension he wants sex again so there is no lasting satisfaction.

It's amazing how a man's energy can change when he makes use of this energy by learning how to control and move it through his body. This same energy as it flows through his body energizes him and causes him to feel more relaxed rather than constantly stressed and tense. Doctors, who deal with medicine, do not explore these facts. Doctors are generally men who have not explored the benefits of relaxation and how it affects the body. Women doctors are not going to explore this field unless they are studying energy and stress levels connected with men releasing their sexual tensions. Therefore, when would women doctors commit themselves to such a study?

These pages contain very valuable information about your health, longevity, and prolonged sexual pleasure. Therefore, you are getting the other half of the picture right here. Perhaps you will find it valuable enough to practice and prove it for yourself?

Always keep in mind that by connecting with your energy at the start of your day through meditation, yoga, tai chi etc, you will maintain balance in your body at all times. Combining this with a program of diet and exercise will give you control and keep you free of illness; this will keep you connected with your internal being, your main power.

To Conclude: When you view Tantra as a method of awakening your spirituality, an inherent part of your sexual energy, you can have a passionate sex life, a healthy and vibrant life, and a healing relationship with your partner. It will also enable you to feel comfortable with your body. It will open your eyes to a new level of sexuality, which includes heightened spiritual awareness, the full dimension of your inner sexual power, and your partner's innermost feelings and desires.

At last perhaps even in our lifetime science may be able to come up with proof how a change in consciousness during sexual bliss or meditation can alter blood structure and strengthen us internally down to our very cell structures, and how this can influence healing and recovery from many illness…. what a blessing !!

In Conclusion

A relationship is based on what is present between two people moment to moment and on subtle messages of the body, breath, and touch. Exploring these realms brings profound delights to any relationship—gentle, loving, sensual play and embrace.

Intimate connections come from knowing your connections to your heart. The freer you are with yourself, the better your energy control will be. As the techniques further enhance your fulfilment and pleasure, you will experience a deeper connection with your soul, and liberated freedom becomes the soul's true expression.

As we are serving the goddess and god within, bringing into play and stimulating the innate love and devotion aspect within us, we bring the divine into our relationships and develop a deeper connection between partners. This allows us to enter a realm of greater openness and freedom. When we are willing to experience such heights that ripple through our bodies we can sustain this experience and carry it into the next day by using the T.O.E. technique.

Bear in mind the reason a woman can feel a greater connection to the goddess energy within herself, as I have previously mentioned, is that it's part of her inherent connection to the divine mother, a natural protector of life all women embody. This enables women to open links for their partners to join them in experiencing this transforming power as sexual energy and experiencing this higher creative power with heightened levels of freedom and ecstasy.

For a man, connecting with his partner on more than just the sexual level lets him experience a deeper connection with his inner power and have full-body orgasmic experiences rather than just genital orgasms. He will gain greater sexual stamina from the balance and harmony this provides his energy and accomplish more in his daily life by using the full-body orgasm practice.

Part of the delight is that you can learn and advance, and your potential for energetic and spiritual growth is never ending. Using this practice daily will give you immediate results, and you will notice a tremendous difference in your relationships and lovemaking within the first few weeks of practice. We all want to be appreciated and loved, and sex is a direct way of expressing this need strongly present in us all.

Never stop exploring and learning about your internal power. The more you learn about yourself, the more control over your life you will have; the only corner of the universe that you can totally change lies within your being. Aldous Huxley said something very similar in his book *Doors of Perception*. No matter what avenue you take, as long as you do whatever you are doing with all your heart, you will succeed.

We are all born with the god source, or "central intelligence," as I prefer to call it. It resides in us as love; as my spiritual teacher John C. King once told me long ago. Because of this, our sole purpose is to recognize and live out of this more fully. Only in this way can we become more human. This is what the ancient text refers to when it says, "the way, the truth, and the light." Because only in this way can we live by the laws of God, which means living in harmony with ourselves. God energy is our soul energy, the internal harmony, and the law of balance. When we have found it in ourselves, we want only to live in harmony with others.

To Conclude : The clearer your energy channel, the more open and powerful you are, hence the importance for you to maintain connection and balance with yourself. By connecting with your power source you discover that all the answers you will ever need, have always been within you, as the pathway to healing and knowledge that we all possess.

Practice every day ftlling your mind with the dream of your lifetime that you want for yourself with all of your heart. Feel delighted as you have set in motion the law of manifesting your dream into reality.

Tatiana

Milton Keynes UK
Ingram Content Group UK Ltd.
UKHW010641040324
438885UK00001B/200

9 781958 381199